P-40 WARHAWK
VS
Bf 109
MTO 1942–44

CARL MOLESWORTH

First published in Great Britain in 2011 by Osprey Publishing,
Midland House, West Way, Botley, Oxford, OX2 0PH, UK
44–02 23rd St, Suite 219, Long Island City, NY 11101, USA

E-mail: info@ospreypublishing.com

OSPREY PUBLISHING IS PART OF THE OSPREY GROUP

A CIP catalog record for this book is available from the British Library.

Print ISBN: 978 1 84908 469 7
PDF e-book ISBN: 978 1 84908 470 3

Edited by Tony Holmes
Cockpit, gunsight, three-view and armament artwork by Jim Laurier
Cover artwork and battlescene by Gareth Hector
Page layout by Ken Vail Graphic Design, Cambridge, UK
Index by Alan Thatcher
Typeset in Adobe Garamond
Maps and diagrams by Bounford.com
Originated by PDQ Digital Media, Suffolk, UK
Printed in China through Bookbuilders

11 12 13 14 15   10 9 8 7 6 5 4 3 2 1

Osprey Publishing is supporting the Woodland Trust, the UK's leading
woodland conservation charity, by funding the dedication of trees.

Acknowledgments
The veterans of the Ninth and Twelfth Air Forces, USAAF, and their family
members who have contributed material to several of my previous books also
made this volume possible. I drew as well from authors, listed in the
bibliography, who have tilled this ground ahead of me, and I truly appreciate
their work. In addition, the Bf 109 photographs provided by Eddie Creek and
Desert Air Force shots from Craig Busby were invaluable. Thanks also to
Andy Szurek for his help with the photographs. Finally, I could not have
completed this book without the Luftwaffe information contained on the
website www.cieldegloire.com.

Editor's note
For ease of comparison please refer to the following conversion table:

1 mile = 1.6km
1lb = 0.45kg
1yd = 0.9m
1ft = 0.3m
1in. = 2.54cm/25.4mm
1gallon (US) = 3.8 liters
1 ton (US) = 0.9 tonnes

P-40 cover art
Supporting the Allied advance against the *Afrika Korps'* Mareth Line in
Tunisia, 36 P-40Ls of the 33rd Fighter Group's three squadrons took off
from Sbeitla on March 30, 1943 to escort 11 B-25s attacking La Fauconniere
airfield, northwest of Sfax – the home of *Jagdgeschwader* 77. When the
Warhawks approached the target area from the west at about 0800 hrs, they
encountered a large force of Bf 109Gs. A whirling dogfight ensued, as noted in
the 58th Fighter Squadron's operations report: "0845–0945, slight haze.
B-25s missed the target, went ten miles beyond, turned and came back. Four
'109s sighted before target, 4–8 after. Capt John R. Bradley was leading the
first flight. He saw four '109s coming in at 30 degrees. He turned into them,
fired a burst and hit one. Maj Levi Chase (60th FS) reported to Bradley that
he saw the enemy aeroplane get hit and crash into the ground". Maj Chase,
flying his P-40L 42-10600, subsequently scored his sixth victory during the
engagement. He would go on to become the top-scoring American P-40 ace
in-theater, with ten confirmed kills. The Warhawk pilots claimed a total of
eight victories for the loss of one P-40 pilot. Apparently, JG 77 suffered no
fatalities during the engagement, although a number of Bf 109s could have
been shot down with their pilots surviving. Oberleutnant Siegfried Freytag and
Feldwebel Hohenberger each claimed single P-40 victories, the former's success
taking his tally to 88 kills. (Artwork by Gareth Hector)

Bf 109 cover art
The first engagement involving Bf 109s and American-flown P-40Fs took place
during the morning of August 14, 1942 when aircraft from JGs 27 and 53 were
scrambled to oppose an incoming Allied bombing mission. Six pilots from the
USAAF's 57th FG were assigned to fly with 12 Kittyhawk Is of No. 260 Sqn
RAF, the fighters providing top cover for 12 South African Air Force Boston
bombers that were targeting airfields in Fuka, on the Egyptian coast. As the
formation crossed the frontlines near El Alamein at about 0630 hrs, 14
Bf 109Fs attacked from out of the sun. Oberleutnant Rudolf Sinner,
Staffelkapitän of 6./JG 27, claimed one victory in his "Yellow 1", Oberfeldwebel
Erwin Sawallisch was credited with two kills and Oberfeldwebel Herbert Krenz
claimed a third victory. American 1Lt William W. O'Neill Jr of the 65th FS,
flying on the wing of Sgt Ron Cundy of No. 260 Sqn, spotted a Bf 109 below
him and broke off to attack it. He soon found himself overwhelmed by five
German fighters, however, and after a brief but fierce fight was forced to bail
out over the Mediterranean. O'Neill landed close to shore and was able to
inflate his dinghy and paddle to the beach in Allied-held territory. In addition
to O'Neill's P-40F, three No. 260 Sqn Kittyhawk Is were shot down in the
engagement. Neither German unit reported any losses. (Artwork by Gareth
Hector)

CONTENTS

INTRODUCTION

When I was a boy growing up in the 1950s, someone told me a tale – perhaps even true – that I have come to see as a fitting metaphor to explain the story of the travails of the pilots who flew the Curtiss P-40 Warhawk against the Messerschmitt Bf 109 during World War II.

It seems that an American metallurgist developed a drill bit roughly the diameter of a human hair that he believed was the smallest in the world. Proud of his accomplishment, the American sent his drill bit to a colleague in Germany to show it off. A few weeks later, the American metallurgist received a package in the mail from his German friend. When he opened it, he found only his drill bit. Curious, the metallurgist examined his drill bit under a microscope and found a hole drilled through it.

Such was the plight of Allied pilots who introduced the P-40 in combat against the Luftwaffe's best in North Africa during 1941–42. Although flying the frontline American fighter of the day, they were thoroughly outclassed in air-to-air combat by the Bf 109s they opposed. The Messerschmitt fighters were faster, had a better rate-of-climb and could fly higher than their Curtiss opponents. Further, the tactics employed by the Luftwaffe pilots took full advantage of the Bf 109's capabilities.

The story does not end there, however. Fortunately for the Allies, the P-40 possessed capabilities of its own that were to prove exceedingly valuable in their effort to drive the Axis powers out of North Africa. The Curtiss fighter was a rugged beast, with heavier armament, longer range and a better turning radius than the Bf 109. Perhaps more importantly, the P-40 could carry a substantial bomb load, which made it a deadly weapon against enemy ground targets when it took on the fighter-bomber role.

This book will focus on the epic duel pitting German-flown Bf 109F/Gs against P-40F/Ls of the US Ninth and Twelfth Air Forces in the Mediterranean Theater from

A P-40F of the 324th FG takes off from a landing ground in Egypt in early 1943. Note how the main landing gear wheels are rotating to tuck into the wings. The markings on this Warhawk are unusual in that it lacks a roundel on the underside of its port wing, and only the nose cone of its propeller spinner has been painted red.

the summer of 1942 through to the spring of 1944, peaking during Operation *Husky* (the invasion of Sicily) in July 1943. It is important for the reader to understand that this is not the full story of combat involving Messerschmitt and Curtiss fighters. In fact, that story goes back to the opening days of the war in September 1939, when earlier versions of the two fighters clashed over France, and ends in May 1945 with the ceasefire on the Eastern Front.

In 1937, as the prospects for war with Germany were growing increasingly likely, leaders of the *Armée de l'Air* in France realized that their domestic aircraft industry would not be able to provide them with sufficient combat-worthy aircraft to effectively oppose their belligerent neighbor. France turned to the American aircraft industry for help and arranged to purchase several hundred export versions of the Curtiss Hawk 75A fighter – the radial-engined predecessor to the P-40. Several units were equipped with these fighters when the war started.

Future ace Sgt Maurice Hards of No. 250 Sqn was an early victim of the Bf 109E-7 when he was shot down in Tomahawk IIB AK374/LD-H north of Sidi Barrani by *experte* Feldwebel Günther Steinhausen of 1./JG 27. Hards had, however, downed another Messerschmitt fighter just minutes earlier.

Two Bf 109F-4/trops of III./JG 53 fly a *freie jagd* over the frontlines near El Alamein, Egypt, during the autumn of 1942. "White 1" may well be the mount of Hptm Wilfried Pufahl of 7./JG 53, who shot down a Kittyhawk for his first victory over North Africa (ninth overall) on May 31, 1942.

Soon after dawn on September 8, 1939, six Curtiss Hawks of *Groupe de Chasse* II/4 were escorting an observation aircraft near Landau-Saargemund when four Bf 109Es from I./JG 53 intercepted the formation. A sharp encounter ensued, and the French pilots claimed two German machines shot down for the first aerial victories of the war by the *Armée de l'Air*. Curtiss Hawks would subsequently prove to be France's most effective fighter during its losing effort in opposition to the German invasion the following spring (see *Osprey Aircraft of the Aces 86 – Curtiss P-36 Hawk Aces of World War 2* for further details).

Likewise, when Great Britain saw the need to bolster its fighter forces in 1940, the Royal Air Force (RAF) ordered Curtiss Tomahawk IIBs, which were export versions of the new P-40B/C then beginning to equip many US Army Air Corps squadrons. Although RAF Tomahawks initially saw action in the tactical reconnaissance role over France, most of the Curtiss fighters acquired by the British were sent to Egypt for service with Desert Air Force (DAF) squadrons.

Tomahawks and Bf 109Es met in combat for the first time on June 16, 1941, when eight aircraft from No. 250 Sqn encountered five fighters from I./JG 27 at 22,000ft over Bardia. The RAF pilots claimed to have damaged two Bf 109Es (see *Osprey Aircraft of the Aces 38 – Tomahawk and Kittyhawk Aces of the RAF and Commonwealth* for further details). The first victory by a Bf 109 over a Tomahawk was claimed by Oberleutnant Ludwig Franzisket of 3./JG 27 over Gazala on June 26, 1941. Luftwaffe fighter pilots would continue to battle the ubiquitous Curtiss fighters, in both USAAF and RAF markings, over the Mediterranean for the next three years.

The Soviet Union also employed large numbers of Tomahawks and Kittyhawks – nearly 2,500 in all – in its war against Germany (see *Osprey Aircraft of the Aces 74 – Soviet Lend Lease Fighter Aces of World War 2* for further details). Apparently, the first combats involving Russian-flown Tomahawks took place in February 1942 against I./JG 54, which was then flying Bf 109Fs from Heiligenbeil, in East Prussia. On March 5, 1942, Feldwebel Gerhard Lautenschläger of 3./JG 54 claimed his fifth Tomahawk shot down, making him the first Luftwaffe pilot of many to reach that total

against the P-40 on the Eastern Front. In May 1945 there was still one regiment of 24 Kittyhawks flying on the Soviet-German front.

Although this book will not cover the foregoing aspects of the P-40 vs Bf 109 duel in detail, they are no less important than the story that I am about to tell. I find inspiration in the courage and perseverance of all those who flew these remarkable aircraft in combat, and the groundcrews who kept them in the air. I hope this book will do justice to them and the sacrifices they made while serving their countries.

Replacement P-40F-5 41-14502, bound for the hard-pressed 33rd FG, takes off from HMS *Archer* on November 14, 1942, just two weeks after the Operation *Torch* landings had opened a second front in North Africa.

Snug in its dispersal pen at Comiso, Sicily, 6./JG 53's Bf 109F-4 "Yellow 12" casts a strong noonday shadow during the summer of 1942.

CHRONOLOGY

1934
March — Design of the Bf 109 commences in response to the issuing of Tactical Requirements for Fighter Aircraft (Land) by Germany's *Reichsluftfahrtministerium*.

1935
May 28 — Maiden flight of Bf 109 V1 is successful.

1936
Autumn — Bf 109 chosen for production over rival Heinkel He 112, having proven superior in speed and maneuverability.

1937
February — Bf 109Bs (first production model of the fighter) issued to II. *Gruppe* of JG 132 "Richthofen".

June 6 — US Army Air Corps (USAAC) issues a contract for production of the Curtiss P-36 monoplane fighter.

1938
Spring — Bf 109C and Bf 109D, both fitted with Junkers Jumo 210 engines, enter production.

October 14 — First flight of the Curtiss XP-40, a modified P-36 airframe fitted with an Allison V-1710 inline engine.

December — Bf 109E-1, fitted with fuel-injected Daimler-Benz DB 601 engine producing markedly improved performance over earlier models, enters service with the Luftwaffe.

1939
April 26 — USAAC orders P-40 into production.

Pilots from 1./JG 27 are distracted during a preflight briefing at a Sicilian airfield in mid-April 1941. The *Staffel* was about to commence the final leg of its flight from Munich to Libya. The pristine Bf 109E-7/trop behind the men wears a freshly applied I. *Gruppe* badge on its nose.

1940
May — P-40D/Kittyhawk I introduced with more powerful Allison "F-series" V-1710 engine, redesigned fuselage and improved armament.

1941
March — Bf 109F-1, with uprated DB 601E engine and other improvements, enters service.

April 14 — I./JG 27, equipped with Bf 109Es, arrives at Gazala to bolster German and Italian air power in North Africa. The Bf 109s go into action five days later.

June 16 — Bf 109Es and Tomahawks encounter each other for the first time, Sqn Ldr J. E. Scoular and Flt Lt R. F. Martin of No. 250 Sqn each claiming a Bf 109E damaged over Bardia.

June 18 — First claims for Tomahawks destroyed by Bf 109E pilots

	Oberleutnant Karl Redlich, Leutnant Hans Remmer and Unteroffizier Günther Steinhausen of I./JG 27.
June 26	First claims for Bf 109s destroyed by Tomahawk pilots Plt Off C. R. Caldwell and Sgt S. L. Coward of No 250 Sqn.
November 25	First flight of the XP-40F, a P-40D airframe fitted with a license-built Packard Merlin V-1650-1 engine.
October 3	II./JG 27, newly arrived with Bf 109Fs, flies its first missions in North Africa. I./JG 27 re-equipped with Bf 109Fs by year-end.
December 7	Japan attacks American military targets at Pearl Harbor, Hawaii, causing the United States to declare war against the Axis powers.

1942

May	III. *Gruppe* first unit of JG 53 to arrive in North Africa.
June	First Bf 109Gs go into action on the Eastern Front.
July	I. *Gruppe* first unit of JG 77 to arrive in North Africa.
July 19	USAAF 57th FG launches 72 P-40Fs from aircraft carrier USS *Ranger* (CV-4) to North Africa.
August 14	Bf 109s encounter USAAF P-40Fs for the first time and shoot down Lt William O'Neill of the 65th FS/57th FG.
September 4	Lt Thomas T. Williams of the 66th FS/57th FG credited with one Bf 109 probably destroyed – the first accepted combat claim by a USAAF P-40 pilot in North Africa.
October 23	British Army opens massive ground offensive against the *Afrika Korps* at El Alamein, in Egypt.
November	Last units of JG 27 depart North Africa, being replaced by II./JG 51.
November 1	P-40F-equipped 324th FG departs US by ship, bound for Egypt.

November 8	Allies commence Operation *Torch*, the invasion of Morocco and Algeria in Northwest Africa. P-40F-equipped 33rd FG flies ashore from the aircraft carrier USS *Chenango* (ACV-28) two days after the invasion.
November 9	Pilots of the 79th FG (second P-40 group to reach North Africa) fly their first combat mission while attached to the 57th FG.
December 6	58th FS/33rd FG goes into action at Thelepte, becoming the first USAAF squadron to operate from an airfield in Tunisia.

1943

January 19	P-40F-equipped 325th FG arrives in Casablanca.
January 23	The Allies capture Tripoli, Libya.
April 18	P-40 pilots of the 57th and 324th FGs claim no fewer than 76 German aircraft destroyed off Cap Bon in the "Palm Sunday Massacre" – the most successful single USAAF fighter mission of World War II.
May 12	Axis forces surrender in Tunisia.
July 9–10	Allied forces invade Sicily. The island is secured 38 days later.
September 3	Allied forces invade southern Italy.
December	P-47 Thunderbolts begin replacing P-40s in the Twelfth Air Force.

1944

May 13	P-40s and Bf 109s meet in combat in the Mediterranean Theater of Operations (MTO) for the last time.
July	Bf 109-equipped JGs 4 and 77 depart MTO for the last time.
July	324th FG, last USAAF P-40 unit in MTO, converts to P-47s.
July 17	Last P-40 lost on combat operations in MTO, the aircraft crashing following an engine fire.

DESIGN AND DEVELOPMENT

P-40 WARHAWK

Built by the company bearing two of the most famous surnames in the early history of powered flight, the P-40 traced its roots to the Curtiss Hawk biplane fighters of the 1920s, starting with the XPW-8 of 1923. Those taper-winged beauties, whether powered by inline or radial engines, were excellent performers that served admirably in US Army and Navy squadrons and were built for export as well. Later versions even featured retractable landing gear.

By the early 1930s the Hawk fighters, and a handful of other successful bomber, observation and attack types, had helped to establish the Curtiss Airplane Division of the Curtiss-Wright Corporation as one of the leading manufacturers of military aircraft in the United States, if not the world. In 1934 – the same year Messerschmitt began working on what would become the Bf 109 – Curtiss initiated the creation of a new monoplane fighter, the Hawk 75. The design team, led by former Northrop engineer Donovan H. Berlin, was instructed to come up with a fighter that could win a USAAC contract competition the following year. Berlin's team created a low-wing monoplane with an enclosed cockpit, retractable landing gear and a 900hp Wright XR-1670 twin-row radial engine.

The Hawk 75 first flew in April 1935 but failed to win the USAAC contract, which went to the Seversky P-35. Three Curtiss service test aircraft were ordered, however, these machines being designated Y1P-36s. Improvements made by the company to the

original H-75 duly impressed the USAAC, and in June 1937 it ordered 210 P-36s from Curtiss. France followed suit with an additional order for 200 fighters.

By all accounts the P-36 was an excellent aircraft, being blessed with a robust airframe, reliable powerplant and lively flying characteristics. In fact, the RAF flew export versions of the aeroplane against the Japanese in Burma well into 1944. But as early as 1938 it became obvious that the P-36's 300mph top speed was not fast enough to allow it to remain competitive with the advanced fighter designs emerging from Europe.

Donovan Berlin went back to work on the H-75 design, replacing the Twin Wasp R-1830 radial engine with a turbo-supercharged version of the new Allison V-1710 liquid-cooled inline powerplant and moving the cockpit aft to offset the additional weight in the nose. The streamlined XP-37 delivered a performance boost as expected, achieving a top speed of 340mph in initial testing. The USAAC ordered 13 service test models of the YP-37, but the experimental turbo-supercharger proved unreliable and sightlines from the cockpit were very poor, so further development of the aeroplane was abandoned. The seed of an idea had been planted, however, a seed that would bloom in the form of the soon-to-be legendary Curtiss P-40.

Berlin returned to the basic P-36 design again for his next attempt to build a high-performance fighter, but this time he took a simpler path. Recognizing that the USAAC believed it needed a fighter that produced maximum performance at an altitude of just 15,000ft, Donovan did away with the complex turbo-supercharging system of the P-37 and simply mated a 1,050hp Allison V-1710-19 engine with conventional supercharging to the airframe of the tenth production P-36A. The new fighter, already designated the XP-40 by the USAAC, had a long, pointed nose similar to the P-37's and the radiator mounted under the fuselage aft of the trailing edge of the wing.

The XP-40 made its maiden flight on October 14, 1938, with Curtiss assistant chief test pilot Ed Elliott at the controls. The aeroplane looked fast, but in initial testing it was unable to top 340mph at 15,000ft. Various tweaks to the design followed, including moving the radiator into a cowling under the nose and replacing the engine with a more powerful V-1710-33, but its speed remained disappointing. The P-40 had other strengths, however. Its handling was generally good, although the aeroplane was not as maneuverable as the P-36, and it had spectacular diving

In June 1937 Curtiss secured the largest single aircraft order placed with an American manufacturer since 1918 when the US Army contracted it to build 210 P-36 Hawks. By the time the first examples reached the 1st Pursuit Group (PG) in April 1938, its performance was, at best, relatively mediocre when compared with fighter designs entering service with air arms in Europe. Nevertheless, the P-36 was blessed with unmatched maneuverability. This particular example was assigned to the 55th PS/20th PG at Barksdale Field, Louisiana, in 1940. The radial-engined P-36 (Hawk 75 in Curtiss nomenclature) was the predecessor to the P-40, sharing the wing and tail designs of the latter aircraft.

speed. Most importantly, it was available. Converting the Curtiss factory from production of the P-36 to the similar P-40 would be a relatively simple task compared to gearing up to build an entirely new aircraft.

By January 1939, when the USAAC held its next fighter competition, tensions were already rising in Europe and the Far East. Despite isolationist sentiment remaining high in the United States, Congress had appropriated funds for a major build-up of the nation's military forces, including the acquisition of a large number of new fighter aircraft.

After comparing the XP-40 to other fighter proposals that were not yet as far along in development such as the Lockheed P-38 and the Bell P-39, the USAAC issued a record-setting contract to Curtiss on April 26, 1939 for 524 P-40s at a cost of nearly $13 million. Although the XP-40 had yet to satisfy the desired performance specifications set out by the Army, the low price and quick availability of the new Curtiss fighter had carried the day. More advanced designs, especially the P-38, promised speed and altitude performance far superior to the P-40, but their manufacturers would require at least two years before they could begin delivering them. Frontline units could start to receive P-40s in half that time, allowing the USAAC to embark on its build-up while Lockheed and other manufacturers developed the next generation of American fighters.

The USAAC chose to skip the option of ordering Y-prefixed service test aircraft and went directly to the P-40 production model. Designated the Hawk 81 by Curtiss, the production model featured the Allison V-1710-33 engine and was armed with four machine guns – two 0.50-in. weapons in the upper cowling and one 0.30-in. gun in each wing.

In December 1939, following months of further airframe "massaging" by Curtiss engineers in the quest for more speed, the modified XP-40 reached 366mph at the desired altitude. This performance duly satisfied the USAAC that the P-40 was indeed sufficiently developed to go into mass production. The first example (39-156) subsequently rolled off the Curtiss production line in March 1940.

This aeroplane, along with the next two off the line, went through a series of tests that determined its top speed was 357mph at 15,000ft, its cruising speed was 277mph and its landing speed was 80mph. The P-40's service ceiling was 32,750ft, and it could climb 3,080ft during the first minute of flight, reaching 15,000ft in 5.3 minutes. Deliveries of the first 200 P-40s to the USAAC began in June 1940. In time, the P-40 would acquire the name "Warhawk" in American service.

Curtiss also began producing an export version of the Hawk 81, which was christened the Tomahawk by the British. France had been the first country to purchase this aircraft, but none of the 185 H-81-A1s that it had ordered in May 1939 had been delivered by the time the nation fell to Germany in June 1940. Great Britain was by then desperate to obtain additional fighters for the RAF, and it accepted the French aircraft, along with placing its own order for Tomahawks.

Sources disagree as to whether Curtiss produced a P-40A or not, but the first significant upgrade to the line was the P-40B, or H-81A-2. The changes in this model were the product of intelligence gleaned from the air battles that had taken place

OPPOSITE
Maj Frederick G. Delany Jr, CO of the 316th FS/324th FG, flew this P-40F-10 on his squadron's first combat mission, on March 26, 1943, in support of the British Eighth Army's final assault on the Mareth Line (on the border of Tunisia and Tripoli). The squadron's P-40s shot up an intersection near El Hamma, leaving six enemy vehicles burning on the road. Despite heavy ground fire, all the P-40s returned safely to base with the exception of Delany's, which was heavily damaged. Badly wounded in the legs, Delany made a forced landing at a British landing ground near the front. He never returned to the squadron due to the severity of his wounds. Delany's P-40F displays the standard 316th FS markings of the period, including the HELL'S BELLES titling and squadron badge on the nose and the Y-prefixed aircraft number on the fuselage. The aircraft's uppersurface desert camouflage, in the Curtiss equivalents of RAF dark earth and middlestone, is in the same pattern applied to export Kittyhawks flown by DAF squadrons.

P-40F-10 WARHAWK

33ft 5.75in.

12ft 4.5in.

37ft 3.5in.

The P-40B was the USAAC's frontline fighter by 1941, when this photograph of 33rd PG aircraft was taken. Curtiss created the P-40 by simply grafting an inline Allison V-1710 engine and cooling system onto the nose of a P-36. The export version of this aircraft, flown by the RAF as the Tomahawk, made its combat debut in the Western Desert in mid-1941.

during the first year of war in Europe. They included refinements such as self-sealing fuel tanks, armor protection for the pilot behind the seat and in the windscreen and the addition of a second 0.30-in. machine gun in each wing. New self-sealing tanks were introduced in the P-40C. These reduced the internal fuel capacity from 160 gallons down to 135, so the provision to carry an external 52-gallon drop tank on the centerline was added in compensation. Each of these items introduced further weight to the P-40, and the performance of the new models – particularly their rate-of-climb – suffered accordingly. Nevertheless, these were the first models of the P-40 that were truly combat-capable.

As previously mentioned, the first P-40s to see combat were the RAF Tomahawk IIBs that went into action in North Africa in June 1941. The strengths and weaknesses of the Curtiss fighter soon made themselves apparent in combat against its German and Italian adversaries. Commonwealth pilots appreciated the Tomahawk as a stable gun platform with a reliable powerplant and a robust airframe capable of absorbing battle damage sufficient to bring down most of its contemporaries. The British replaced the 0.30-in. wing guns with their own 0.303-in. weapons to simplify supply problems, and pilots found this armament sufficient for desert warfare. The Tomahawk's maneuverability and speed in the dive also were found to be competitive with the Bf 109E/Fs and Macchi C.202s that it met in combat.

No USAAF-assigned P-40Es made it to the MTO, although the virtually identical Kittyhawk I/IA was a staple fighter for DAF units in 1941–42. The bulk of the E-models assigned to American fighter groups saw combat in the Pacific and China-Burma-India (CBI) theaters. This particular P-40E served as a backdrop for pilots from the Hawaii-based 72nd PS/15th PG in early 1942.

The Tomahawk's major shortcoming for desert combat was its poor performance at higher altitudes. Ranking Allied Tomahawk/Warhawk ace Australian Clive Caldwell, who scored 20.5 victories in Curtiss fighters, noted that while they performed creditably in a dogfight if operating within their own altitude limitations, their pilots were forced to leave the initiative with their higher-flying opponents. In order to engage the enemy at the Tomahawk's best height, pilots had to accept the fact that they must endure an initial attack from above, then turn into their protagonists and bring their heavy armament to bear in a head-on pass.

Fighter pilots of at least eight different nations flew P-40s and Tomahawks during the H-81's operational combat life. Perhaps the most famous of these aeroplanes were the 100 Tomahawks diverted from the British in 1941 to equip the American Volunteer Group (AVG) in Burma and China.

While the Curtiss factory was busy turning out P-40s and Tomahawks, Allison engineers were developing a more powerful version of the V-1710 engine. The 1,150hp Allison "Series F" (V-1710-39) was initially slated for a new Curtiss fighter, the XP-46, but the USAAC did not want to shut the company's production lines down long enough for them to convert to the new machine. Curtiss, meanwhile, had redesigned the P-40 with the new engine to fill a British order in May 1940. The USAAC also purchased 22 examples of the new H-87A Kittyhawk as the P-40D in September 1940, and soon followed this up with orders for no fewer than 820 P-40Es.

The H-87A was a major departure from the earlier models, with a completely new fuselage. A change in gearing moved the thrust line of the V-1710-39 engine (and thus the center of the propeller spinner) up so that it was nearly in line with the exhaust stacks. With the higher line of thrust, the fuselage was shortened by 6.75 in. and the radiator/oil cooler chin scoop was deepened. The upper section of the fuselage was cut down and a larger cockpit opening gave the pilot improved vision.

Armament also changed in the H-87A. The nose guns were removed and four 0.50-in. weapons were installed in each wing, along with an improved system of hydraulic gun chargers. The nearly identical H-87A-3/P-40E featured six 0.50-in. wing guns, with 281 rounds of ammunition per weapon. A 500lb bomb or 52-gallon drop tank could be fitted on the centerline shackle and six 20lb bombs mounted to attachments on the undersides of the wings.

The improvements in the P-40D/E did not translate into significantly better speed or altitude performance when compared to previous models, however. Top speed was 355mph at 15,000ft, and the service ceiling actually dropped to 29,000ft. Range was a respectable 800 miles at normal cruising speeds and 1,150 miles at 195mph.

When a supply of Rolls-Royce-designed Merlin engines became available in 1941, a P-40D was modified to accept the powerplant made famous in the RAF's Spitfire and Hurricane fighters. Designated the P-40F/Kittyhawk II, the new version had a slightly different nose that featured a deeper chin inlet and lacked the air scoop on top of the cowling. Partway through its production run of 1,311 airframes, the P-40F got a 26in. rear fuselage extension to improve directional stability. This feature carried

A 64th FS/57th FG armament crew prepares to attach two 250lb bombs to the centerline shackles of a P-40F at Scordia, in Sicily, in September 1943. Armorers used innovation and sheer will to adapt available ordnance to fit attachment points on their aircraft. Note the drop tank that was previously mounted to the Warhawk's centerline lying in the background at right.

over to the P-40L, which Curtiss attempted to lighten by deleting two wing guns and other equipment.

The Merlin 28 engines, built in the USA by Packard, featured a single-stage, two-speed supercharger that offered a modest improvement to the aircraft's performance at altitude when compared to the Allison-engined variants. Other than that, the performance of the P-40F/L was similar to earlier models.

The next Allison-powered H-87, the P-40K/Kittyhawk III, featured an improved Allison V-1710-73 and an enlarged vertical tail – another attempt to solve directional stability problems. This aircraft also got the 26in. fuselage extension late in its production run, and the similar P-40M that followed it had this feature too.

The last major version of the H-87, and the most numerous, was the P-40N/Kittyhawk IV series. With this variant, which was powered by the same Allison V-1710-81 that equipped the P-40M, Curtiss engineers took the lightening efforts started in the P-40L several steps further, and in the process produced the fastest production model with a top speed of 378mph. Various improvements were introduced in the eight sub-variants of the P-40N that followed, the most visible of these being the N-5's modified cockpit canopy with a frameless sliding hood and cut-down rear fuselage. This became a standard fit for all subsequent versions of the N-model.

The last Warhawk, P-40N-40 serial number 44-47964, rolled out of the Curtiss factory on November 30, 1944, completing a production run of 13,738 aircraft.

Bf 109

Of all the iconic fighters of World War II, the Messerschmitt Bf 109 stands alone as a symbol of its nation, for its superiority in the war-torn skies of Europe waxed and then waned in synch with the fortunes of Germany. Conceived amid controversy by Willy Messerschmitt's Bayerische Flugzeugwerke AG in 1934, the small fighter would go on to be manufactured in greater numbers than any other aircraft in history save one, the Soviet Il-2 *Shturmovik*.

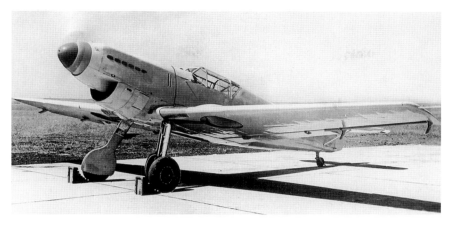

The initial prototype Bf 109 V1 D-IABI won the Luftwaffe's 1935 fighter trials while powered by an imported Rolls-Royce Kestrel engine. Not only was the fighter a great performer, its design would also prove to have tremendous development potential and easy adaptability to mass production.

Just three months after Adolf Hitler assumed power in Germany, the *Reichsluftfahrtministerium* (RLM) took a crucial step toward creating a new German air force when, on July 6, 1933, it issued a document titled Tactical Requirements for Fighter Aircraft (land). Considering the date, the RLM set a high bar for the new single-seat fighter that would equip the Luftwaffe. The aeroplane would need to be able to maintain 250mph for 20 minutes at 20,000ft, climb to that altitude in 17 minutes and attain a maximum altitude of 33,000ft. It had to be equipped with two machine guns or a single cannon, plus a radio, an oxygen system and a cockpit heater. Operationally, the fighter needed to dive and turn well, be able to take off and land from an average Luftwaffe airfield with an average German pilot at the controls and be small enough to be transported by rail.

The question facing the RLM was whether Messerschmitt's company, which had no experience in building military aircraft, should be allowed to compete for the lucrative fighter contract. After all, Arado, Focke-Wulf and Heinkel had already built fighters for the Luftwaffe, while Bayerische Flugzeugwerke AG's sole claim to fame was the highly advanced Bf 108 Taifun, a high-speed sport aeroplane with low-set cantilever wings. In the end, Messerschmitt was able to secure a development contract from the RLM, and his engineers got to work incorporating the successful features in the Taifun – leading-edge slats to improve low-speed handling, slotted flaps and an enclosed cockpit – to the new Bf 109 design.

The square wingtips of the Bf 109E are clearly visible in this shot of an "Emil" and its pilot from 7./JG 26 – the first Luftwaffe single-engined fighter unit to be deployed to the Mediterranean. Reaching Sicily in early February 1941 under the command of Oblt Joachim Müncheberg, the "Red Heart" *staffel* quickly established the superiority of its Bf 109E-7s over the Hurricane defenders on Malta, then moved on to North Africa in May.

From the beginning, the Bf 109 was envisioned as the smallest possible airframe that could be fitted with the most powerful available engine. Its aluminium monocoque fuselage, built in two halves and joined along the centerline, was an oval in section. Its width was as narrow as the dimensions of the engine and the shoulders of an average pilot would allow. This streamlining was seen as a great advantage during the Bf 109's development, as it produced an aircraft capable of great speeds.

However, it would ultimately prove to be more of a hindrance, as the cramped space allowed no room for increasing fuel capacity or armament as dictated by combat experience without adding various bumps, pods and droppable exterior items that compromised the fighter's streamlined shape.

One unusual aspect of the fuselage design was the pilot's seating position, which was inclined somewhat compared to the normal chair-type seat in which the pilot's torso was vertical. This gave the Bf 109 an advantage over other fighters in high-speed maneuvering because the G-forces on the pilot pulled more front-to-back than top-to-bottom, thus reducing the loss of blood from the brain that induces gray-outs and blackouts.

The prototype Bf 109 V1 was rolled out of Bayerische Flugzeugwerke AG's Augsburg plant in September 1935, the aircraft being powered by a Rolls-Royce Kestrel V engine because Messerschmitt had been unable to obtain one of the new Junkers Jumo 210A engines. Test flights were successful, and the sleek fighter was delivered to Travemunde for evaluation in October. There, much to the surprise of the German aviation establishment, the Bf 109 clearly out-flew the Arado Ar 80 and Focke-Wulf Fw 159, while performing at least as well as the Heinkel He 112 but with more speed. As a result, contracts to produce ten aircraft each were issued to Bayerische Flugzeugwerke AG and Heinkel. Subsequent development would establish the Bf 109's superiority over the He 112.

Now with access to the Junkers Jumo 210 inverted V12 engines, Bayerische Flugzeugwerke AG completed the next two prototypes by June 1936. These aircraft were lightly armed as per the RLM specifications, but already word was filtering in from England about the multi-gun armament that was to be installed in the new Hurricane and Spitfire fighters that

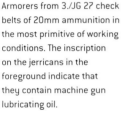

were then under development. It was decided that the new Bf 109B would boast three Rheinmetall 7.92mm MG 17 machine guns, including one firing through the propeller spinner. When supplies of the Oerlikon MG FF/M 20mm cannon became available, these would replace the engine-mounted gun. The first pre-production Bf 109B-0 was completed in early 1937.

The outbreak of civil war in Spain on July 17, 1936 would have a profound effect on the future success of the Bf 109 in air combat. Fascist leader Gen Francisco Franco soon called on Germany and Italy for military assistance, which both were happy to provide. Seeing a chance to field-test their new weapons under combat conditions, the Germans organized the *Legion Condor* for service in Spain. The Bf 109 V3-V6 prototypes were shipped out directly from operational trials in early 1937, and within a year Bf 109B-1, B-2 and C-1 fighters equipped three *staffeln* of *Jagdgruppe* 88. The Bf 109E also joined the fray in early 1939.

The pilots and technical advisors of J 88 spent more than two years in Spain developing tactics and techniques that would give the Germans a distinct edge over their Allied opponents in the early stage of the world war that was soon to follow.

The Bf 109E was a major improvement on the Jumo-engined B-, C- and D-models that preceded it. Developed from the Bf 109 V14, the E-model featured the 1,100hp Daimler-Benz DB 601A engine with direct fuel injection and advanced supercharging. Armament was also improved, with two MG 17 machine guns in the upper cowling and two MG FF cannons in the wings. The aircraft's performance – 354mph at 12,300ft, a rate-of-climb of 3,100ft per minute and a service ceiling of 36,000ft – made the earlier models instantly obsolete. Soon, sub-versions would emerge, including the E-1/B fighter-bomber and further models with improvements in armament, powerplant and equipment.

With the Bf 109E, dubbed "Emil" by its pilots, the Luftwaffe had a world-class fighter with which to go to war. When Germany invaded Poland on September 1, 1939, the Luftwaffe had 12 fighter *gruppen* equipped with 850 Bf 109E-1s and E-1/Bs. The quick victory over the Polish air force gave the Luftwaffe scant opportunity to assess the superiority of its fighter force, but subsequent successes over the Low Countries and France in the spring of 1940 convinced Bf 109 pilots that they were flying the best fighter in the world.

It was not until Germany attempted to subdue Great Britain by air attack in the summer of 1940 that the Bf 109's primary shortcomings came into play for the first time. As expected, the "Emil" acquitted itself well against RAF Spitfires and Hurricanes during the opening engagements of the Battle of Britain, which took place primarily over the English Channel and along the south coast. But the Bf 109's short range meant that it could only spend 20 minutes over England, which severely hampered operations as the Luftwaffe bombers began ranging farther inland. Furthermore, the requirement placed on Bf 109 pilots midway through the battle to provide close escort to the increasingly beleaguered bomber formations negated the aggressive hunting tactics they preferred and placed them in the role of hunted instead.

The Bf 109E-4, which reached the frontline during the Battle of Britain, introduced the more powerful DB 601N engine, revised armament and a squared-off

OVERLEAF
Bf 109G-6/trop "Yellow 16" of 9./JG 53 was one of the many "Gustavs" left behind by the Luftwaffe when it hurriedly withdrew from North Africa in May 1943. The fighter had been landed by a mortally wounded pilot, a single 20mm cannon shell having gone through the upper longeron on the left side of the fuselage and exploded in the cockpit. Another round had penetrated the left side of the fuselage and exploded against the laminated aluminium armor-plate behind the cockpit. Discovered abandoned in a wheat field near the airstrip at Mateur, in Tunisia, by members of the 325th FG, the aircraft was quickly restored to flying condition by American mechanics. Repainted matt black overall, with a red spinner, rudder and ailerons, and marked with "stars and bars", the fighter carried the name *Hoimann* in a Gothic typeface on the nose. American pilots flew the aeroplane to familiarize themselves with its characteristics, and in one memorable flight Lt Col Bob Baseler buzzed a neighboring P-38 airfield in the "Gustav" to protest several incidents of Lightning pilots firing on the 325th's P-40s, having mistaken them for Bf 109s.

Bf 109G-6/TROP

29ft 7in.

8ft 2.5in.

32ft 6.5in.

cockpit canopy, giving the pilot a better view of the sky. The E-5 and E-6 mounted cameras for the reconnaissance role, while the last major "Emil" variant, the E-7, was basically an E-4 with the provision to carry a 66-gallon drop tank. It saw extensive service in the Balkans and the Mediterranean.

By the time Germany invaded the USSR in June 1941, the "Emil" was being phased out of service in favor of the Bf 109F. The "Friedrich", as the F-model was called, wrapped the 1,200hp DB 601N engine in a streamlined new cowling, added rounded wingtips for an increased wingspan and omitted the "Emil's" bracing struts under the horizontal stabilizer. The result was a sleeker Bf 109 with a substantial increase in performance. Top speed was now 390mph at 22,000ft, rate-of-climb was 3,200ft per minute and the service ceiling jumped to 37,000ft.

Luftwaffe pilots embraced the "Friedrich's" flight capabilities but were less enthusiastic about its armament, which reverted to three guns grouped in the nose. The F-1 featured a single 15mm cannon mounted between the cylinder banks of the engine and firing through the propeller spinner plus two rifle-caliber machine guns in the upper cowling. With the F-4 came a switch in cannon to the 20mm version of the MG 151. A "Jabo" fighter-bomber version of the F-4 was also produced.

The "Friedrich" served as the Luftwaffe's primary fighter through to late 1942, and many of the Luftwaffe's top *experten* considered it to be the best fighter-versus-fighter version of the entire Bf 109 line. From the channel coast of France to the wastes of western Russia and the barren landscape of North Africa, Bf 109F pilots shot down Allied aircraft by the thousands. But combat requirements were changing, as the first daylight raids on Germany by heavy four-engined bombers of the US Eighth Air

6./JG 53's Bf 109F-4 'Yellow 2" was photographed at Comiso, Sicily, in early December 1941, the unit having only just arrived in the Mediterranean from the Eastern Front. The famous "Pik-As" ("Ace of Spades") *Geschwader* would see considerable action over Malta and North Africa with its "Friedrichs" through to the autumn of 1942, when the unit began to receive Bf 109G-2s.

Messerschmitt production lines turned out more than 24,000 Bf 109Gs from mid-1942 through to the end of the war. This staggering total was half again as large as the production run of the USAAF's most numerous fighter, the Republic P-47 Thunderbolt.

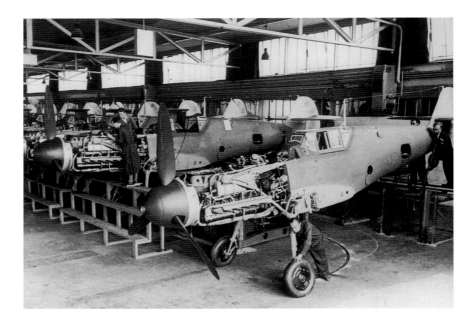

Force sent a hint of things to come. The Luftwaffe introduced a second fighter, the outstanding Focke-Wulf Fw 190, while Messerschmitt engineers continued to massage the nine-year-old Bf 109 design. Next up was the Bf 109G, or "Gustav".

Destined to be manufactured in far greater numbers than any prior version of the Bf 109, the "Gustav" outwardly resembled the "Friedrich" when the first models rolled off the production line in June 1942. The heart of the Bf 109G was a new engine, the DB 605A-1, producing 1,475hp – and even more than that with the GM 1 nitrous-oxide power boosting system. This was desperately needed too, as the Bf 109 continued to put on weight. The G-6 model, for example, weighed 5,900lb when empty, compared to 4,330lb for the F-3.

Climbing to 19,000ft now required six minutes. Maximum speed of the new model remained about the same (387mph at 22,900ft for the G-6), as did the service ceiling of 39,000ft. The heavier Bf 109s were tricky to fly at slower speeds, and their narrow landing gear – never a strong part of the Bf 109 design – gave inexperienced pilots fits. Maneuverability also suffered, especially when the "Gustavs" were equipped with underwing cannon pods or rocket launchers (effective weapons against heavy bombers), which added both weight and drag.

Numerous modifications were made to the Bf 109G series, most of which were incorporated into the G-6. This model carried heavier 13mm MG 131 machine guns in the cowling, which necessitated "blisters" on the upper fuselage skin to clear the larger breech blocks of the new guns. These "buelen" (boils) became the key identifying features of late-model Bf 109Gs.

Introduced to frontline Luftwaffe units in North Africa in late 1942, the "Gustav" also served in Italian fighter squadrons and was the last of the Bf 109 line to engage in combat with the P-40. A further version, the Bf 109K, was introduced in October 1944, although it primarily equipped Defense of the Reich units.

TECHNICAL
SPECIFICATIONS

P-40

P-40/TOMAHAWK I

Aircraft in the first batch of 199 production P-40s were not truly combat-worthy, as they lacked armor plating and self-sealing fuel tanks. Fortunately, the USA had not yet entered the war when the first P-40s were delivered. Powered by an early version of the Allison V-1710 liquid-cooled V12 engine, they were fitted with two 0.50-in. machine guns in the nose and one 0.30-in. weapon in each wing. The French ordered a similar model, designated the H-81-A1, which was armed with four 0.30-in. wing guns instead of two. Most of these were taken over by the RAF as Tomahawk Is in mid-1940 after France fell. They were employed by the RAF primarily as trainers or stored for future shipment overseas.

P-40B–C/TOMAHAWK II

The first upgrade of the P-40 line addressed many of the shortcomings of the previous model. Improvements included armor protection for the pilot, upgraded radio equipment and the addition of a second 0.30-in. machine gun in each wing. The P-40C added self-sealing fuel tanks and the provision to carry a drop tank or bomb on a centerline station below the cockpit. Many P-40B/Cs found their way to USAAC squadrons in the Philippine Islands and Hawaii, thus becoming the first Warhawks to

The export version of the P-40B/C for the RAF was the Tomahawk II. Here, AH775 of No. 268 Sqn banks away from the camera over southern England to reveal the sleek lines of its nose, with the radiators grouped under the engine drawing air through a streamlined scoop. The four 0.303-in. machine guns in the wings supplemented two heavier 0.50-in. weapons in the nose.

see action in American markings. The British version of these aircraft, fitted with 0.303-in. wing guns but otherwise similar, was used for low-level fighter-reconnaissance sorties over occupied Europe and in fighter-bomber operations in North Africa. Some 100 Tomahawk IIBs were diverted in 1941 from the British order to the Chinese Air Force, where they would equip the legendary AVG, soon to be known worldwide as the "Flying Tigers".

P-40D–E/KITTYHAWK I

When Allison redesigned its V-1710 to produce the upgraded "F-series" engine, Curtiss needed to rework the P-40's fuselage so as to accommodate the higher thrust line and additional horsepower of the new powerplant. The guns were duly removed from the redesigned nose, Curtiss replacing the four small-caliber wing guns with 0.50-in. weapons in the P-40D. The armament was increased to six 0.50-in. weapons in the E-model, as it was in late-build Kittyhawk Is and all Kittyhawk IAs. The new fuselage also introduced an improved cockpit transparency, with a bigger windscreen and deeper sliding canopy. A further model for the USAAF, the P-40E-1, could carry six small 40lb bombs under the wings, and late in its production run a small dorsal fillet was added at the base of the vertical stabilizer to improve longitudinal stability. P-40Es and Kittyhawk Is saw extensive combat in the Pacific, China-Burma-India and in North Africa.

P-40F/KITTYHAWK II

In an attempt to improve the performance of the P-40 at higher altitudes, Curtiss fitted a P-40E airframe with a Rolls-Royce Merlin engine, the same powerplant as in the Spitfire and Hurricane. The engine, license-built by the Packard Motor Company and equipped with a two-stage mechanical supercharger, gave the P-40F a top speed of 364mph at 20,000ft. The nose was redesigned to remove the air scoop on top of the cowling because the Merlin engine was fitted with an updraft carburetor. This meant that the powerplant drew its air through an enlarged radiator scoop below the engine. In an effort to further improve the stability of the Warhawk, Curtiss extended the rear of the fuselage by 26in. from the 700th P-40F onwards. Because they were considered better able to cope with high-flying German and Italian fighters, most P-40Fs and Kittyhawk IIs were sent to American and Commonwealth squadrons fighting in the MTO.

P-40K/KITTYHAWK III

Outwardly, the P-40K-1 and K-5 Warhawks were identical to the late-production P-40E-1s, with the small dorsal fillet at the base of the vertical stabilizer and flared exhaust pipes fitted to the engine. But there was a big difference under the cowling. Curtiss gave the P-40K a considerable boost in performance over the previous Allison-engined models with the 1,325hp V-1710-73. The added power made the P-40K the fastest Warhawk yet, even outpacing the P-40F at 20,000ft. The armament remained six 0.50-in. guns in the wings. With the P-40K-10 and -15, Curtiss went to the 26in. fuselage extension introduced on the late-model P-40F. These were the first P-40s fitted with a radio antenna mast on the fuselage spine. Two squadrons within the 57th FG flew P-40Ks from late 1942 through to the end of the North African campaign. The RAF received 192 Kittyhawk IIIs through Lend-Lease and most of them served in the MTO with Commonwealth air forces.

Armorer Daryl Benson of the 66th FS/57th FG USAAF loads 0.50-in. ammunition into one of the wing boxes of the P-40F flown by his squadron commander, Maj Charles Fairlamb, in the autumn of 1942. The standard armament throughout the production run of the P-40F was six guns, and the aeroplane also could carry bombs.

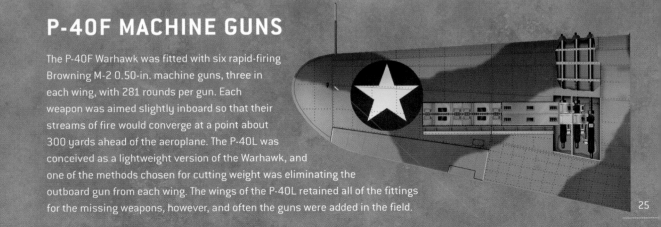

P-40F MACHINE GUNS

The P-40F Warhawk was fitted with six rapid-firing Browning M-2 0.50-in. machine guns, three in each wing, with 281 rounds per gun. Each weapon was aimed slightly inboard so that their streams of fire would converge at a point about 300 yards ahead of the aeroplane. The P-40L was conceived as a lightweight version of the Warhawk, and one of the methods chosen for cutting weight was eliminating the outboard gun from each wing. The wings of the P-40L retained all of the fittings for the missing weapons, however, and often the guns were added in the field.

Seen shortly after its arrival in North Africa, and prior to being issued to a frontline unit, this P-40L-10 was written off in a crash on October 31, 1943.

P-40L/KITTYHAWK II

Seeing no further prospects for a significant boost in engine power any time soon, Curtiss began to strip weight from the Warhawk in the P-40L. This model was basically a Merlin-powered P-40F with several items removed or modified – armament was reduced to four 0.50-in. wing guns, less armor plate was fitted and internal fuel capacity dropped from 157 gallons to 120. These changes lopped about 140lb from the empty weight compared to the P-40F. A very slight improvement in performance over the F-model resulted, but the loss of combat effectiveness was keenly felt by pilots in the frontline. The P-40L-1 retained the short fuselage of the early P-40F, but the 650 P-40Ls with serial numbers starting at 42-10480 had the 26in. fuselage extension. L-models supplied to the RAF were designated Kittyhawk IIs, like the P-40Fs before them. As the end of the P-40F/L production runs drew near in spring 1943, the USAAF decided that the new North American P-51B Mustang fighter should have the top priority for Merlin engines. This decision left no fewer than 300 P-40F/L airframes lacking engines, and these were converted to Allison power and re-designated P-40Rs.

When P-40F losses began to mount in the MTO in the autumn of 1942, K-model Warhawks were supplied to groups in-theater as attrition replacements from November of that year. These aircraft were powered by the 1,325hp Allison V-1710-73 engine, which limited their combat effectiveness to an altitude of about 20,000ft. This factory-fresh example was photographed at Heliopolis, in Egypt, from where it was sent to the 57th FG.

Like the P-40E, the lightweight and long-tailed P-40N also failed to reach USAAF Warhawk units in the MTO, although some saw action with RAF squadrons in Kittyhawk IV form. This particular N-model was assigned to the 23rd FG's 74th FS at Hengyang, in China, in mid-1944.

P-40M/KITTYHAWK III

Throughout the P-40's life, Curtiss was trying to develop a new fighter to replace the Warhawk in frontline service. The company's P-46 and P-60 designs failed to make it into production, however, and the USAAF still needed fighters. An order for 600 new P-40M Warhawks resulted, with deliveries starting in November 1942. Outwardly, the P-40M was little changed from the long-tailed P-40K, but it got a new Allison engine in the form of the 1,200hp V-1710-81. Because the P-40M was so similar to the P-40K, the RAF designated both aircraft Kittyhawk IIIs.

P-40N/KITTYHAWK IV

The last production version of the Warhawk, the P-40N, was a further attempt to cut weight from the by now veteran fighter. In all, 5,210 P-40Ns were built in nine sub-versions, making it the most numerous of all Warhawks, and also the most varied. The first version, the P-40N-1, was outwardly similar to the P-40M except that its armament was reduced to four wing guns. The P-40N-5 and later models had an improved cockpit transparency and reverted to six wing guns. Most of the 458 Lend-Lease Kittyhawk IVs went to New Zealand and Australia for service in the Pacific, although some saw action with RAF squadrons in the MTO.

Bf 109
Bf 109B, C and D

The early production versions of the Bf 109, starting with the B-1, evolved rapidly during the late 1930s. Initially powered by a Junkers Jumo 210 inverted V12 engine producing up to 730hp, the Bf 109D graduated to the superior 960hp Daimler-Benz DB 600. Likewise, the three-blade VDM propeller debuted on the Bf 109D.

The Bf 109B was the first production model of Messerschmitt's famous fighter. Fitted with a 640hp Junkers Jumo 210 E engine driving a two-bladed variable-pitch propeller, the Bf 109B-2 had a top speed of 279mph at 13,100ft with a full military load.

Armament grew from the B-1's three 7.9mm MG 17 machine guns to the C- and D-model's four guns, with two in the wings and two in the upper cowling. Early attempts to mount a 20mm cannon firing through the propeller hub did not work, as the airframe shuddered when the gun was fired and the weapon usually jammed after a few rounds. This problem was solved in later versions, and it became a staple of the Bf 109 design. All three subtypes served in Spain and were the dominant fighter of the conflict. The *Legion Condor's* top scorer was Werner Mölders, who scored 14 victories with the Bf 109C-1.

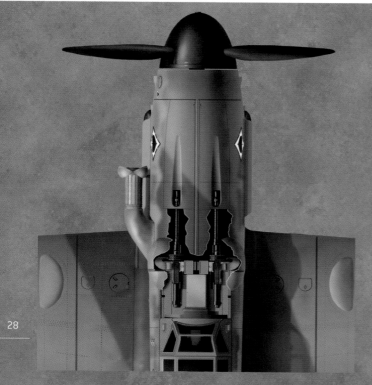

Bf 109G MACHINE GUNS

Designed with air-to-air combat operations in mind, the Bf 109G grouped all of its weapons in the nose to give their rounds line-of-flight trajectory. This advantage was somewhat offset by the fact that the aircraft carried just three guns, compared to the Warhawk's six. Like the Bf 109F before it, the "Gustav" was initially fitted with a pair of Rheinmetall MG 17 7.92mm machine guns in the nose. However, from the G-6 variant onwards, these were replaced by harder-hitting MG 131 13mm machine guns. Each weapon had a magazine holding 300 rounds mounted just forward of the cockpit. The MG 131s were synchronized with the engine to avoid damaging the propeller when they were fired.

Bf 109E-7/trop

The complexion of the air war in North Africa changed completely when the first elements of I./JG 27 arrived at Gazala in April 1941. Within days, its Bf 109E-7/trops established their superiority over the Hurricane fighters flown by the RAF at that time. With a DB 601A engine developing 1,175hp, the E-7 was nearly identical to the E-4. It was armed with two 20mm MG FF/M cannons in the wings and two 7.9mm MG 17 machine guns in the upper cowling, and it could also carry a 66-gallon drop tank or bombs under the fuselage. Internal drop tank connections, a bomb-release mechanism and related wiring were factory installed, allowing units to convert from long-range fighter operations to fighter-bomber duties in the field. Messerschmitt prepared the "Emil" for tropical service through the fitment of a dust filter over the supercharger's air intake and the inclusion of an emergency desert survival kit.

Bf 109F-2/trop and F-4/trop

Bf 109Fs arrived in North Africa with II./JG 27 in late 1941. The "Friedrich" was generally considered by Luftwaffe pilots to be the best flying variant of the entire Bf 109 series. Some pilots initially balked at its reduction in armament to one cannon and two machine guns, but they were soon won over by the improved speed (390mph) delivered by the 1,300hp DB 601E and cleaned-up airframe, plus the gain in maneuverability provided by the new wing. Both the F-2/trop and F-4/trop were fitted

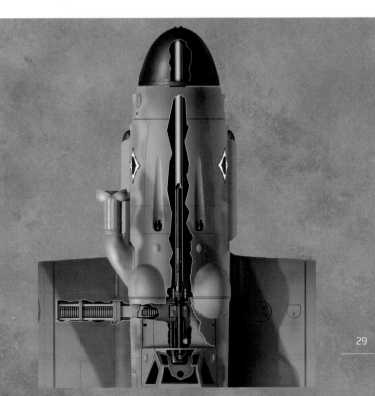

Bf 109G ENGINE-MOUNTED CANNON

As with earlier versions of the Bf 109, the "Gustav" also featured an engine-mounted automatic cannon – either a 20mm Mauser MG 151/20, with a magazine holding 200 rounds of ammunition, or a 30mm Rheinmetall MK 108 with a 60-round magazine. Because the muzzle of the cannon protruded through the center of the propeller hub, the gun did not require synchronization. Later models of the Bf 109G also mounted two more 20mm Mausers in gondolas beneath the wings. Although these guns greatly increased the firepower of the aircraft, they adversely affected its speed and maneuverability.

with a canister-type air filter to keep desert sand and dust out of the engine. The key difference between the two was the re-barreled centerline MG 151 cannon in the F-4, which had an increased caliber (up from 15mm to 20mm) but a reduced rate of fire (650 rounds per minute). The Revi C/12C reflector gunsight was also standard equipment on the Bf 109F, assisting many Luftwaffe fighter pilots in boosting their scores of enemy aircraft destroyed. These were simple sights, without computing aids to assist the pilot. They did, however, feature a built-in dimmer to regulate the intensity of the reticule, plus the fitting of "sun dark" glass to reduce glare. An auxiliary optical sight was fitted in the cockpit as well in case the Revi were to fail. Later, the C/12D gunsight gave pilots bomb-aiming capability in addition to fixed gunnery. Versions of the Reflexvisier (abbreviated to "Revi") gunsight dated all the way back to the Bf 109B.

Bf 109G-2/trop

With the introduction of the "Gustav" in the late summer of 1942, the Bf 109 began the transition from the fighter-versus-fighter role to an anti-bomber weapon. Although very similar outwardly to the F-model, the "Gustav" featured a more powerful engine in the form of the 1,475hp DB 605. The only exterior clues to tell an early G-model from an F are the addition of two small intake scoops aft of the propeller spinner and

P-40 AND Bf 109 COMPARISON SPECIFICATIONS		
	P-40F-10	**Bf 109G-2**
Powerplant	1,300hp Packard Merlin XX V-1650	1,475hp Daimler Benz DB 605 A-1
Dimensions		
Span	37ft 3.5in.	32ft 6.5in.
Length	33ft 5.75in.	29ft 7in.
Height	12ft 4.5in.	8ft 2.5in.
Wing area	236 sq. ft	174.37 sq. ft
Weights		
Empty	6,300lb	5,893lb
Loaded	8,368lb	6,834lb
Wing loading	35.46lb/sq. ft	39.19lb/sq. ft
Performance		
Max speed	364mph at 20,000ft	406mph at 28,540ft
Range	750 miles	528 miles
Climb	to 15,000ft in 7.6 min.	to 19,000ft in 6 min.
Service ceiling	34,400ft	37,890ft
Armament	6 × 0.50-in. Brownings	2 × 7.9mm MG 17s 1 × 20mm MG 151/20

the deletion of triangular windows below the side panels of the windscreen as part of the fitment of the cockpit pressurization system in the G-1. The G-2 was not pressurized but was otherwise similar. It was not uncommon to see these aircraft equipped with underwing MG 151/20 20mm cannon pods or even WGr 21 mortar launchers to increase their punch against enemy bombers. The addition of these weapons significantly reduced the "Gustav's" speed and maneuverability, placing it at a disadvantage when confronting Allied fighters.

Bf 109G-6/trop

The G-6 "Gustav" was essentially an unpressurized G-5. The main difference between these aircraft and previous G-models was the replacement of the MG 17 cowl-mounted guns with MG 131 13mm weapons. To accomplish this, Messerschmitt had to modify the fuselage by adding substantial "buelen" (bumps) to cover the large breech blocks of the guns. Also, some of the late-build G-6s carried a powerful center-mounted MG 108 30mm cannon in place of the smaller MG 151/20. More than 12,000 Bf 109G-6s were produced between late autumn 1942 and June 1944.

THE STRATEGIC SITUATION

By the time the first American fighter pilots went into action in Egypt in August 1942, the P-40 and Bf 109 had already been in steady combat over the Western Desert for a year. But the air war in North Africa went back even longer than that. The seesaw battle for control of North Africa started in June 1940 when Italy declared war on Great Britain. RAF squadrons in Egypt immediately launched attacks against Italian forces in neighboring Libya.

At that time, biplane fighters equipped both sides, with Gloster Gladiators being flown by British units (see *Osprey Aircraft of the Aces 44 – Gloster Gladiator Aces of World War 2* for further details) and Fiat CR.42s by their Italian counterparts (see *Osprey Aircraft of the Aces 90 – Fiat CR.42 Aces of World War 2* for further details). The British soon deployed more modern Hurricane I monoplane fighters to Egypt and the strategic island of Malta. Although only available in limited numbers, the Hurricanes quickly achieved air superiority for the time being.

The ground war began in earnest in September 1940, when the Italian army advanced eastward into Libya, emboldened by Germany's successes in northern Europe. Within two months the Italian advance had stalled, and the British counterattacked in December. By early 1941 the British had advanced nearly 1,000 miles to El Agheila, capturing more than 100,000 Italian troops in the process. At that point Germany entered the desert conflict to head off further disaster for its Italian allies. German General Erwin Rommel and his soon-to-be-famous *Afrika Korps* attacked in April 1941, and within two weeks British forces had been pushed all the way back into Egypt. There, a stalemate developed, as German resources were diverted to the impending attack on the Soviet Union.

At first the Luftwaffe had sent only Ju 87 Stuka dive-bombers, an assortment of medium bombers and Bf 110 twin-engined escort fighters to the Mediterranean theater. However, in an attempt to overwhelm the defenses on Malta, the first Bf 109s joined the fight in February 1941. Some 14 Bf 109E-7s of 7./JG 26 began flying patrols over the island from its base on Sicily, wreaking havoc on the weak Malta air defenses. Further fighter support for the Axis forces arrived in April 1941 when Bf 109E-equipped I./JG 27 began flying sorties from Ain El Gazala Landing Ground (LG) in Libya. Its 90 fresh fighters, clearly superior to the DAF's aging Hurricane Is, quickly changed the complexion of the air war over North Africa.

With its aircraft industry stretched to supply a two-front war, Great Britain turned to the United States for help. Soon, American-built Martin Maryland II medium bombers and Curtiss Tomahawk IIB fighters were headed to the Middle East for service with the DAF. The first squadron to equip with the Tomahawk was newly formed No. 250 Sqn, which arrived at Amriya, in Egypt, on May 12, 1941 to provide air defense for the port city of Alexandria. This squadron scored the first confirmed victory for the P-40 series on June 8, 1941 when Flg Off "Jock" Hamlyn shot down an Italian Cant Z.1007 bomber while on patrol.

The Bf 109E-7/trop debuted in North Africa with I./JG 27 in April 1941 and immediately found success in air combat over the Libya-Egypt border. "Yellow 4" of 3. *Staffel* wears the olive dapple-over-tan camouflage scheme and white fuselage identifier band common among the first "Emils" to fly in North Africa. The distinctive unit badge of I. *Gruppe* is visible on the forward cowling.

The second unit in the DAF to receive Tomahawk IIBs was No. 3 Sqn RAAF, which flew its first mission with the new fighter on June 8, 1941. This aircraft, squadron code letter "I", shows evidence of having its factory dark earth/dark green European upper camouflage colors converted to the desert scheme by simply overspraying the dark green portions with middlestone.

33

The DAF had adopted a red propeller spinner for its fighter force by the time this photograph of No. 260 Sqn Kittyhawk IIIs was taken in Libya in late 1942. FR358/HS-B was flown by one of the great aces of North Africa, Flt Lt "Eddie" Edwards. The aircraft nearest to the camera was also the mount of an ace, squadron CO, Sqn Ldr "Pedro" Hanbury.

The first encounter between Tomahawks and Bf 109s took place on June 16, when eight aircraft from No. 250 Sqn and five "Emils" of I./JG 27 clashed over Bardia at 1500 hrs. Two Tomahawk pilots claimed to have damaged Bf 109s, but there were no losses suffered by either side. On June 18 four Bf 109s jumped a formation of No. 250 Sqn Tomahawks returning from a strafing mission and shot down three, victory credits going to future aces Oberleutnant Karl-Wolfgang Redlich, Leutnant Hans Remmer and Unteroffizier Günther Steinhausen. Eight days later No. 250 Sqn claimed its first Bf 109s destroyed when future ranking P-40 ace Flg Off Clive Caldwell and Sgt George Coward were each credited with one apiece.

An improved Curtiss fighter, the Kittyhawk, began to arrive in December 1941, No. 3 Sqn RAAF being the first unit to re-equip. The Kittyhawk's main advantage over the Tomahawk was its improved firepower of six wing-mounted 0.50-in. machine guns.

The British mounted a second major ground campaign late in 1941, and by mid-January 1942 they again were deep inside Libya. Once more, their success was fleeting, however, for Rommel struck back on May 26, 1942 at Gazala. Soon British forces had been pushed all the way back to El Alamein, in Egypt, which was less than 100 miles west of Alexandria.

Just as Rommel's advance was gaining pace, British Prime Minister Winston Churchill arrived in Washington, D.C., to discuss war plans with the US president, Franklin D. Roosevelt. Early on, the two leaders had agreed on a "Europe first" policy for the defeat of the Axis powers. American-made war materials were being shipped across the Atlantic at a ferocious pace, but thus far Roosevelt had been reluctant to commit US combat forces to the European conflict piecemeal. He preferred to build up American forces to sufficient strength to open a second front on the continent with one smashing blow. Now, however, with the British backed up in Egypt again and

Soviet leader Josef Stalin demanding relief from the German invasion of his country as well, Roosevelt agreed to commit American units to North Africa. Among them would be six fighter groups of the USAAF, the first of which was to be operational in-theater by September 1, 1942. That group would be the 57th FG.

Equipped with 75 new Merlin-powered P-40F Warhawks, the 57th FG took off from the aircraft carrier USS *Ranger* (CV-4) on July 19, 1942 and proceeded across Africa to Palestine. There, the group would fly a number of practice missions under the tutelage of combat-experienced RAF instructors. While training proceeded in Palestine, small groups of 57th FG pilots began moving up to the frontlines in Egypt to gain actual combat experience with the DAF. These pilots, initially unit commanders and flight leaders, were assigned to Kittyhawk and Tomahawk squadrons. They would fly as wingmen to combat veterans during their first fighter-bomber sorties over the Western Desert – nicknamed "The Blue" by DAF veterans. Here, in the barren lands west of the Nile River, they would fight for nearly a year.

The 57th FG's first orientation missions took place on August 9, 1942, and five days later American pilots encountered enemy aircraft for the first time. On the morning of August 14, six pilots of the 57th FG were assigned to fly with the RAF's No. 260 Sqn, which was in turn providing top cover for 12 South African Boston bombers attacking airfields in Fuka, on the Egyptian coast.

These were the locations of Luftwaffe Bf 109 and Desert Air Force P-40 units on the eve of the last Allied advance from El Alamein. With their superior range, the P-40 fighter-bombers were able to strike ground targets far behind enemy lines during the ensuing campaign, while the Bf 109s served primarily as point defense interceptors.

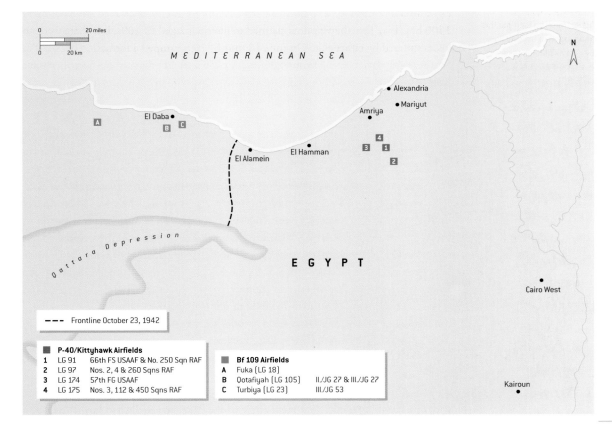

P-40/Kittyhawk Airfields
1 LG 91   66th FS USAAF & No. 250 Sqn RAF
2 LG 97   Nos. 2, 4 & 260 Sqns RAF
3 LG 174   57th FG USAAF
4 LG 175   Nos. 3, 112 & 450 Sqns RAF

Bf 109 Airfields
A Fuka (LG 18)
B Qotafiyah (LG 105)   II./JG 27 & III./JG 27
C Turbiya (LG 23)   III./JG 53

--- Frontline October 23, 1942

Oblt Rudolph Sinner flew this Bf 109F at Martuba during the first half of 1942 whilst serving as technical officer of JG 27. Made *Staffelkapitän* of 6./JG 27 during the summer of that year, Sinner would shoot down what was almost certainly the first P-40F lost by the USAAF in North Africa for his 24th victory on August 14. In a case of mistaken identity, he claimed that his victim was a "Curtiss P-46", a developmental design that never reached production.

As the formation crossed the frontlines near El Alamein, 14 Bf 109s attacked from out of the sun and a whirling dogfight ensued. 1Lt William W. O'Neill Jr of the 65th FS, flying on the wing of Sgt Ron Cundy, spotted a Bf 109 below him off to the right and he broke formation and attacked it. He soon found himself overwhelmed by five more German fighters, however, and after a brief but fierce fight the American was forced to bail out over the Mediterranean Sea. O'Neill landed close to shore and was able to inflate his dinghy and paddle to the beach in Allied-held territory. On returning to his unit O'Neill reported that he had shot down two Bf 109s, but his claims were never officially recognized. Victories were credited to Oberleutnant Rudolph Sinner, Oberfeldwebel Erwin Sawallisch (two) and Oberfeldwebel Herbert Krenz of II./JG 27. Three pilots from III./JG 53 also submitted damaged claims.

I./JG 27's Oberleutnant Hans-Joachim Marseille, the Luftwaffe's "Star of Africa", was credited with no fewer than 101 Curtiss fighters destroyed in 1941–42.

The American P-40 pilots continued to gain experience over the next two months, scoring their first victories and suffering their first fatalities. On the other side of the El Alamein front, Bf 109 pilots were continuing to run up their scores, but they too were taking losses. Far in the lead was Hauptmann Hans-Joachim Marseille, dubbed by the Berlin press the "Star of Africa". *Staffelkapitän* of 3./JG 27, Marseille had been credited with an astonishing 158 victories (including no fewer than 101 P-40s, Tomahawks and Kittyhawks) by the time his luck ran out on September 30, 1942.

Whilst he was on patrol behind Allied lines in a new Bf 109G-2/trop, Marseille's engine caught fire. Encouraged by his fellow pilots to nurse his blazing machine back over German-held territory despite his cockpit filling with smoke, Marseille then tried to bail out when the fighter rolled over into a steep dive. As he fell away from the stricken machine, Marseille struck the tailplane of his "Gustav" with his chest, the blow

Some 35 P-40F Warhawks of Detachment J, the so-called "Joker Squadron", pack the deck of the British aircraft carrier HMS *Archer* on November 9, 1942 while en route to North Africa. These machines were shipped directly from Floyd Bennett Field, New York, as attrition replacements to make good the losses suffered during the Operation *Torch* landings.

knocking him unconscious and leaving him unable to deploy his parachute. The great *experten* duly fell to his death on the desert floor.

At first light on October 24, some 230,000 men of the British Eighth Army began moving forward from El Alamein in three distinct thrusts against the 107,000 Italian and German troops facing them. Above the front, creating an umbrella over the Allied troops and a hailstorm of bombs and bullets for the enemy, were massed formations of DAF bombers and fighters. No. 211 Group boasted seven Kittyhawk squadrons and one unit still flying Tomahawks, plus three squadrons each of Spitfires, Hurricanes and 57th FG Warhawks. A further eight Hurricane squadrons flew in No. 212 Group, and nine bomber units were equipped with Bostons, Baltimores and USAAF B-25 Mitchells. The primary Axis fighter forces opposing the Allied pilots were the three *gruppen* of the Luftwaffe's JG 27 and one from JG 53, flying Bf 109F/Gs, plus seven Italian *gruppi* equipped with Macchi C.202s.

The P-40F Warhawks of the 57th FG flew three missions on the opening day of the offensive, each time escorting Boston bombers, but had only one inconsequential

2Lt Thomas T. Williams of the 56th FS/57th FG was flying this P-40F-1 (41-13970) on September 4, 1942 when he scored the USAAF's first official air-to-air claim in the MTO – a Bf 109 probably destroyed. Shown here in about December 1943 after it had picked up the name *COUNT PISTOFF* and RAF fin flashes, "White 95" was shot down on January 11, 1943, carrying its regular pilot, Lt W. B. "Bill" Williams, to his death.

37

An *Alarmstart* (emergency scramble) for pilots of 4./JG 53 at La Marsa, in Tunisia, in March 1943. "White 4" was the mount of *Staffelkapitän* Oblt Fritz Dinger, who claimed five P-40s destroyed between April 18 and July 27, 1943. He was killed by bomb shrapnel during a raid on Scalea airfield on the latter date, his victory tally having by then reached 67. JG 53 extracted a fearsome toll on Allied air power during its losing battle to hold Tunisia, claiming nearly 300 victories before the Axis surrender on May 12, 1943.

encounter with enemy fighters. A midday mission by the 64th FS on October 25 brought the initial victory for the pilot who would later become the 57th FG's first ace, 27-year-old New Yorker 1Lt Lyman Middleditch Jr. In little more than a week, Rommel's forces began to withdraw westward, with the Eighth Army in hot pursuit. Thus began the next phase of war in "The Blue", a 1,400-mile chase across Libya and Tunisia that would continue until the following spring.

As the frontlines shifted westward, the P-40 and Kittyhawk squadrons moved as well so as to remain within range of the fighting. Before the end of the North African campaign, the 57th FG would move some 34 times to new airfields as the Allied advance pressed farther west, completing the trek at Cape Bon, Tunisia, in June 1943. In addition, two more USAAF fighter groups equipped with P-40s – the 79th FG and, later, the 324th FG – were sent to Egypt for assignment to the DAF.

Allied landings in Morocco and Algeria on November 8, 1942 opened a second front in North Africa, and further complicated the defensive challenge facing Axis forces. Among the American units committed to Operation *Torch* was the 33rd FG of the Twelfth Air Force, equipped with 77 P-40Fs. Two days after the invasion, the 33rd FG flew its Warhawks off the deck of the carrier USS *Chenango* (ACV-28) and landed at Port Lyautey, Morocco. The quick capitulation of the Vichy French defenders left the P-40 pilots with little to do until the first week of December, when the 58th FS flew to the newly captured airfield at Thelepte, Tunisia, to commence combat operations. The group was heavily engaged for the next two months, flying offensive missions and also defending its base against enemy air attack – on 15 January 1943, the 59th FS claimed eight Ju 88s destroyed.

The 33rd FG had just 13 flyable Warhawks left when it pulled out of Thelepte on February 8 to rest and re-equip with new P-40Ls, returning to action in Tunisia in

A groundcrewman of the 64th FS/57th FG poses in the cockpit of 1Lt R. J. "Jay" Overcash's P-40K-1 42-46040 "White 13" at Hani Main, Tunisia, soon after the pilot had scored his final two kills to "make ace" on the afternoon of April 26, 1943. All five of his victims were Bf 109s.

mid-March. A major encounter on March 30 with Bf 109Gs of JG 77, which had been flying in North Africa for nearly a year, was one of several fierce combats that occurred through early April. A second P-40 group, the 325th FG, joined the Twelfth Air Force at about this time and began combat operations in April.

Pressured from the east and west, the *Afrika Korps* held out in Tunisia until May 13, 1943, when all Axis forces remaining in Africa surrendered. By this time the Allies were already making plans for the invasions of Sicily and then Italy. These massive operations would provide the backdrop for the decisive showdown between P-40s and Bf 109s in the MTO.

2Lt MacArthur Powers of the 314th FS/324th FG and another pilot make a low pass over an airfield in Egypt in early 1943. A future ace, Powers transferred to the USAAF after scoring 2.25 victories flying Spitfire VBs with the RAF's No. 145 Sqn during 1942.

THE COMBATANTS

PILOT TRAINING

Fascination with the exploits of the ace fighter pilots of World War I and the civilian airmen who broke aviation boundaries postwar was an international phenomenon among boys who grew up in the 1920s and 1930s. This was particularly true in the developed nations, American boys soaking up the stories of Rickenbacker and Lindbergh, while in Germany the heroes were von Richthofen and Udet. With millions of young men eager to emulate their aviation heroes as their nations prepared for war in the late 1930s, the air forces of Germany and the United States were able to set high standards for intelligence and physical condition in their pilot recruits.

The terms of the 1919 Treaty of Versailles banned military aviation in Germany, but by the late 1920s the nation was already finding ways around the restriction. By the time the Luftwaffe (the air arm of the Wehrmacht) was formed in 1935, Germany had a ready supply of airmen that had been trained under the guise of civilian enterprises. These men received strict training in the Prussian military tradition to prepare them for service as officers and NCOs in the Luftwaffe. Many of them flew in Spain and then took part in the opening campaigns of World War II.

By late 1940, when the United States began to seriously gear up for war, Germany was already suffering combat attrition in its fighter units. As the demand for new pilots grew, the Luftwaffe compressed its training system into a program that emphasized flying skills and turned out qualified pilots in 10 to 13 months. Future pilots started in a flight training regiment where they received basic military tuition and preliminary aviation education. Three to four months of basic flight instruction

Five Fw 44 biplane trainers sit on the flightline at a Luftwaffe training base. Known as the Stieglitz ("Goldfinch"), the Fw 44 was produced by Focke-Wulf as a pilot training and sport flying aircraft from 1932.

followed in biplane trainers such as the Fw 44 Stieglitz and the He 72 Kadett. Those who showed promise went on to Pilot School A/B, which included elementary aerobatics instruction to help identify potential fighter pilots among the students. Pilots chosen for fighter training moved ahead to fighter school for about 50 hours of further instruction on obsolescent fighter types, including early-model Bf 109s.

Nineteen-year-old trainee Heinz Knoke recalled his painful introduction to the Bf 109 at No. 1 Fighter School on October 12, 1940 in his postwar memoir, *I Flew for the Führer*:

> This morning we brought out the first '109 and were ready to fly. Sgt Schmidt was chosen as the first of us by drawing lots. He took off without difficulty, which was something, because the aircraft will readily crash on take-off if one is not careful. A premature attempt to climb will cause it to whip over into a spin, swiftly and surely. Schmidt came in to land after making one circuit, but he misjudged his speed, which was higher than that to which he was accustomed, and so he overshot the runway. He came round again, and the same thing happened. We began to worry, for Sgt Schmidt had obviously lost his nerve.

Luftwaffe student pilots practice formation flying in Arado Ar 96A trainers. Used for advanced, night and instrument flying training, the Ar 96 was a single-engine, low-wing monoplane of all-metal construction.

P-40F/L WARHAWK COCKPIT

1. N-3A reflector gunsight
2. Ring gunsight
3. Flap and wheel indicator
4. Compass
5. Artificial horizon
6. Coolant temperature gauge
7. Fuselage fuel gauge
8. Turn and bank indicator
9. Turn indicator
10. Airspeed indicator
11. Tachometer
12. Manifold pressure gauge
13. Oil temperature gauge
14. Engine gauge unit

15. Rate-of-climb indicator
16. Altimeter
17. Clock
18. Propeller circuit breakers
19. Oil pressure gauge
20. Landing gear warning light
21. Parking brake
22. Gun arming switch
23. Radio contactor
24. Carburetor heat control
25. Canopy control crank
26. Throttle
27. Mixture control
28. Propeller control

29. Ignition switch
30. Compass control
31. Ammeter
32. Cockpit heat control
33. Rudder trim tab control
34. Elevator trim tab control
35. Fuel selector
36. Rudder pedals
37. Control column
38. Gun firing button
39. Wing tanks fuel gauge
40. Hydraulics hand pump
41. Radio receiver
42. Radio transmitter

43. Map case
44. Fluorescent spotlight
45. Wing bomb release
46. Pilot's seat
47. Cowl flaps control
48. Radio crash switch
49. Filter switch box
50. Flap control
51. Undercarriage selector handle
52. Oxygen regulator
53. Windscreen defroster pump
54. Fuel suction gauge
55. Rearview mirror

Bf 109G-6/trop COCKPIT

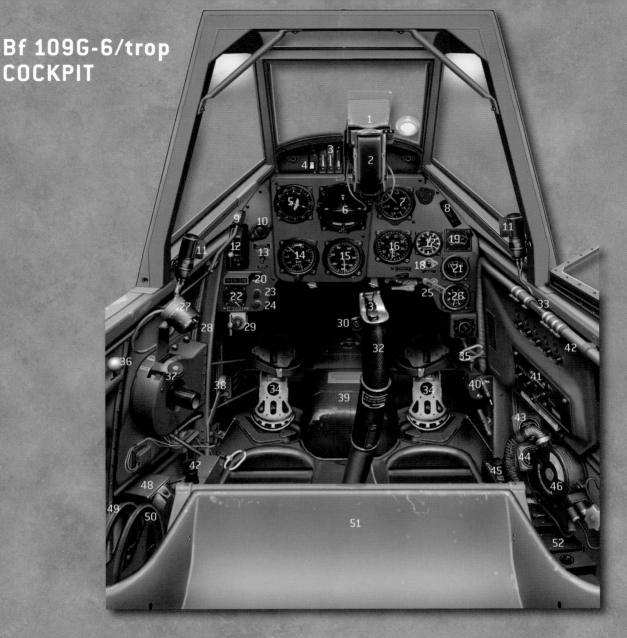

1. Revi C/12D reflector gunsight
2. Gunsight pad
3. Ammunition counters
4. Armament switch
5. Repeater compass
6. Artificial horizon/turn-and-bank indicator
7. Manifold pressure gauge
8. Tumbler switch
9. Canopy jettison lever
10. Main light switch
11. Instrument panel light
12. Ignition switch
13. Start plug cleansing switch
14. Altimeter
15. Airspeed indicator
16. Tachometer
17. Propeller pitch position indicator
18. Fuel warning lamp
19. Combined coolant exit and oil intake temperature indicator
20. Starter switch
21. Fuel gauge
22. Undercarriage position indicator
23. Undercarriage "up" light
24. Undercarriage "down" light
25. Undercarriage emergency release lever
26. Oil and fuel content gauge
27. Throttle
28. Propeller pitch control
29. Dust filter handgrip
30. Bomb release button
31. Gun firing trigger
32. Control column
33. Auxiliary fuel contents indicator
34. Rudder pedals
35. Radiator cutoff handle
36. Ventilation control lever
37. Oil cooler flap control
38. Fuel cock lever
39. MG 151/20 cannon breech cover
40. Radiator shutter control lever
41. FuG 16ZY radio control panel
42. Drop tank pipe
43. Oxygen supply indicator
44. Oxygen pressure gauge
45. Radio control
46. Oxygen supply
47. Fuel injection primer pump
48. Tailplane incidence indicator
49. Undercarriage emergency lowering handwheel
50. Tailplane trim adjustment wheel
51. Seat
52. Radio tuner panel

Although the Vultee BT-13 was officially christened the Valiant by the USAAF, it was known as the "Vibrator" to most trainees because of its peculiar shaking while in flight. The BT-13 entered service in 1939, and with more than 11,000 built, it was the USAAF's most numerous basic trainer of World War II.

He was coming in and making a final turn before flattening out to touch down when the aircraft suddenly stalled because of insufficient speed and spun out of control, crashing into the ground and exploding a few hundred feet short of the end of the runway. We all raced like madmen over to the scene of the crash. I was the first to arrive. Schmidt had been thrown clear and was lying several feet away from the flaming wreckage. He was screaming like an animal, covered in blood. I stooped down over the body of my comrade and saw that both his legs were missing. I held his head. The screams were driving me insane. Blood poured over my hands. I have never felt so helpless in my life. The screaming finally stopped and became an even more terrible silence. Then the others arrived, but by that time Schmidt was dead.

About an hour later, Knoke successfully completed his first flight in a Bf 109. He would go on to fly more than 400 missions and score 52 victories over the Eastern Front and during the Defense of the Reich.

The frontline *geschwader* provided operational training for fighter pilots prior to assigning them to combat units. At the time of his posting to a *staffel*, a fledgling Luftwaffe fighter pilot would have about 200 hours of flying time to his name.

The P-40 pilots who squared off against the Bf 109 in the Mediterranean during 1942–43 were the products of similar training to the post-Battle of Britain Luftwaffe *jagdflieger*. After completing preparatory military training, which could last for several months, USAAF student pilots commenced their flying lessons in primary school on docile training aircraft, mostly biplanes such as the Stearman PT-17. One of the main purposes of primary training was to weed out those who showed no talent for flying, but the students who graduated went on to the next level, called "basic" training in the USA. Here the standard training aircraft for USAAF pilots was the Vultee BT-13/15, a low-wing monoplane with fixed landing gear. Trainees flew the much-admired North American AT-6, a monoplane with retractable landing gear, in their final training phases, called "advanced".

An American pilot would receive his wings and officer's commission after about nine months of instruction and 200 hours of flight time. In the pre-war years, he

Most American military pilots of World War II — Army, Navy and Marines — flew the North American AT-6/SNJ during advanced flight training. As the Harvard, this same aircraft also took part in the training of thousands of Commonwealth pilots. Here, two AT-6s fly close formation over the Alabama countryside in 1941.

would then be assigned to an active squadron, where his piloting skills would continue to develop while flying first-line combat aircraft. In December 1942 the USAAF instituted Fighter Replacement Training Units (FRTU) to give newly minted fighter pilots experience in the types of aircraft they would be flying in combat. The FRTU courses, normally about two months in duration, included instrument training and night flying, air-to-air and air-to-ground gunnery instruction and practice in formation flying and combat maneuvering.

Initially, the great difference between USAAF and Luftwaffe fighter pilots when they initially met in combat was the experience levels of the officers who led them. When the 57th FG flew its first sorties in August–September 1942, its mission leaders had no more combat experience than did the "tail-end charlies". They were all learning their trade together. By contrast, during that period the 57th FG regularly went up against JG 27 formations led by pilots whose experience dated back to the Battle of Britain, if not earlier. The DAF attempted to blunt this disadvantage for the 57th FG by assigning its flight leaders to fly with experienced RAF Kittyhawk squadrons for their first few missions.

One advantage enjoyed by USAAF fighter groups was having the opportunity to fly frontline fighter types during their final phase of training while providing air defense in the USA prior to shipping out for a combat zone. These P-40Fs of the 314th FS/324th FG are on alert at Baltimore, Maryland, in the summer of 1942.

When their operational days ended, many early model Bf 109s continued to serve the Luftwaffe in the training role. Pilots chosen for fighter training went on to fighter school for about 50 hours of further instruction on obsolescent single-seat types, and the first flight in a Bf 109 was always a challenge for them.

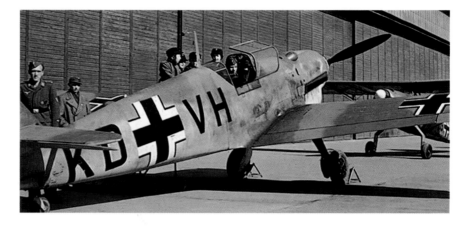

Similarly, the opportunity for an inexperienced Bf 109 pilot to watch and learn from *experte* such as Hans-Joachim Marseille, Hans-Arnold Stahlschmidt and Werner Schroer (who claimed 331 victories between them) must have given him a leg up on his P-40 counterpart when they first met in the skies over western Egypt.

It was not until mid-1943, when tour-expired P-40 pilots with extensive combat experience began showing up as instructors in fighter training units back in the USA, that the experience factor began to tip in favor of the Americans. Then in early 1944 Luftwaffe fighter pilot training was shortened to an average of 160 flight hours. A few weeks later it was further shortened to just 112 hours. Finally, in the late spring of 1944, the B flight schools were disbanded and pilots were sent into frontline service directly after A school. In order to achieve A2 flight certification, German pilots now had to complete only 60 flights totaling 15 hours during basic training. Meanwhile, the average USAAF or RAF fighter pilots would continue to receive 225 flight hours throughout the war.

For the most part, USAAF P-40 units in the MTO used a "Finger Four" formation that was a direct copy of the standard Luftwaffe fighter formation. However, the 57th FG also used a formation that it borrowed from the RAF called the "Fluid Six". This formation replaced the side-by-side leader-wingman combination, being based instead on three front-and-back pairs of fighters that could provide mutual cover and support. The pairs were stacked in altitude so that the pair flying up-sun and covering the tails of the leaders (Nos 1 and 2) flew higher, while the down-sun pair flew lower. In theory, any attacking aircraft could be sandwiched between two pairs of P-40s, no matter the direction or altitude of the attack.

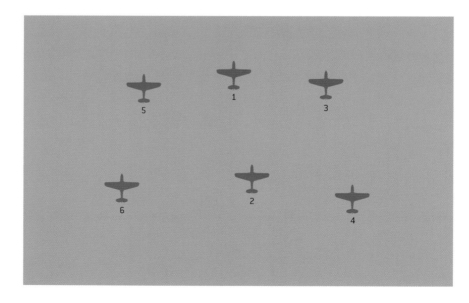

LEVI R. CHASE JR

Levi Chase was born in Cortland, New York, on December 23, 1917. Entering the US Army in November 1940, he was subsequently accepted as an aviation cadet. As a member of Class 41-G, he received his pilot's wings and commission as a second lieutenant in September 1941 at Maxwell Field, Alabama. Initially assigned to the 8th Pursuit Group (PG), Chase joined the 33rd PG's 58th PS, equipped with Warhawks, on December 22, 1941.

Flying a P-40F off the aircraft carrier *Chenango* on November 10, 1942, Chase had his first taste of combat during the invasion of North Africa in November 1942. Newly promoted to captain, he scored two kills flying with the 58th – his first a Bf 109 on December 18 and then a Ju 88 four days later. Eventually made CO of the 33rd FG's 60th FS (and having been promoted to major) Chase continued to run up his score, downing six Bf 109s, an Fw 190 and a C.202 between January 31 and April 5, 1943. Completing his combat tour with the 33rd FG in July 1943, Chase returned home as the USAAF's ranking Warhawk ace in the MTO.

After a year in the USA Chase deployed to Burma with the 2nd Air Commando Group. He later became commander of the P-51D-equipped 1st Provisional Fighter Group and was credited with downing two Japanese Army Air Force Ki-43 "Oscars" in March 1945.

Following World War II, Chase entered civilian life, but he was recalled to active duty in April 1951 and served in Korea as commander of the 8th Fighter-Bomber Wing, flying F-80s and F-86s.

From December 1952 until 1964, now-Col Chase attended both the Air War College and the National War College, and served in several command and senior staff positions throughout the USA and in Germany. In 1964, he successively commanded the 15th and 12th Tactical Fighter Wings at MacDill AFB, Florida – the first two wings in the USAF to become combat ready with the F-4C Phantom II. In October of the following year Chase led the 12th Tactical Fighter Wing to Cam Ranh Bay Air Base, Republic of Vietnam, remaining in-theater until October 1966. Later, he served as vice-commander of the 313th Air Division at Kadena Air Base, Okinawa, and as Chief of the Air Section of the Military Assistance and Advisory Group in Taiwan, Republic of China.

Gen Chase returned to the USA in July 1969 to become the Tactical Air Command Assistant Deputy Chief of Staff for Operations, and in July 1971 he was made deputy commander of the Ninth Air Force, assuming command in 1973. Maj Gen Levi Chase finally retired in November of that same year following 33 years of military service. He died in Cortland, New York, on September 4, 1994.

ORGANIZATION

The operational units of the USAAF and Luftwaffe were organized along similar lines. The numbered air forces of the USAAF corresponded to the Luftwaffe's *Luftflotten* ("air fleets"), and both were assigned to specific geographical areas. In the MTO, the USAAF's Ninth Air Force supported the westward advance from Egypt, and the Twelfth Air Force took part in the Operation *Torch* invasion of Morocco and eastward advance into Tunisia. The Ninth Air Force headquarters subsequently moved to England following the Axis surrender in North Africa, leaving its units behind to be incorporated into the Twelfth Air Force. Germany's *Luftflotte* 2 controlled its air operations in the Mediterranean throughout this period.

The basic operational units (squadrons and *staffeln*) were controlled by the group in the USAAF and the *geschwader* in the Luftwaffe. A USAAF group, commanded by a colonel or lieutenant colonel, normally consisted of three or four squadrons further broken down into several flights. On paper, a USAAF fighter squadron would be equipped with about 25 aircraft and pilots. Its basic tactical formation was four flights of four aircraft each. Full group formations of P-40s were sometimes seen on bomber escort missions in the MTO. A common configuration for dive-bombing missions was one squadron of P-40s carrying bombs while a second Warhawk unit provided top cover in an effort to protect the vulnerable fighter-bombers from being bounced by high-flying Bf 109s over the target area. The number of fighters participating in sweeps, patrols, interceptions and reconnaissance flights varied down to a basic element of two P-40s.

A Luftwaffe *geschwader* was commanded by a *geschwaderkommodore*, who held the rank of oberst (colonel), oberstleutnant (lieutenant colonel) or major. The

This new P-40F-1 (41-14295) of the 87th FS/79th FG was photographed at El Kabrit, in Egypt, on January 29, 1943 while the group received its final training prior to going into action in March of that year. The fighter's two-tone camouflage was factory-applied on late production F-1s bound for North Africa. The 79th FG used the letter prefix "X" to distinguish its machines from those of the 57th FG. Note also the newly applied red propeller spinner and RAF fin flash – both standard markings for all aircraft serving with the DAF.

jagdgeschwader (fighter wing) usually consisted of three *gruppen* (groups), which in turn consisted of three *jagdstaffeln* (fighter squadrons). Hence, *Jagdgeschwader* 27's first *gruppe* was I./JG 27 and its first *staffel* (squadron) was 1./JG 27. In addition, a *stabschwarm* (headquarters flight), usually numbering up to six aircraft, was attached to each *geschwader* and *gruppe*. *Geschwader* strength was supposed to be 120–125 fighters, but this number was extremely fluid – and often substantially smaller as the war progressed.

TACTICS

Although the P-40 flew on every front during World War II, it is best known as the mount of the AVG, popularly known as the "Flying Tigers", who gained fame in 1941–42 for their successes against the Japanese in Burma and China. The AVG's dive-and-zoom tactics, devised by brilliant "Flying Tiger" commander Claire Lee Chennault, utilized the P-40's superior capabilities – primarily diving speed and firepower – to counter the more maneuverable but lightly armed and constructed Japanese fighters.

However, Chennault's tactics were of no use to P-40 units in the MTO. Pilots of the *Legion Condor*, led by Werner Mölders, had developed tactics very similar to Chennault's soon after the Bf 109 joined the conflict in Spain during the late 1930s. In the Mediterranean, the German pilots had the superior aircraft to utilize these tactics because the Bf 109's service ceiling was much higher than the P-40's. Their strategy was to climb to high altitude, wait for the enemy to appear below them and

Although used to operating from unprepared grass strips, German fighter pilots found that the sandy "airfields" in North Africa, which were strewn with rocks the size of house bricks, were something else entirely. The biggest handicap of all was the dust cloud thrown up by any kind of aircraft movement. This aerial photograph of a *Schwarm* taking off – each of the four widely spaced machines trailing its own lengthening plume of dust and sand – illustrates the extent of the problem.

49

JOACHIM MÜNCHEBERG

A well-known athlete in his youth and a natural leader, as well as a gifted fighter pilot, Joachim "Jochen" Müncheberg rose from flight cadet to *kommodore* of JG 77 in just five years, and had scored 135 victories by the time he lost his life in combat with American fighters on March 23, 1943. His victory tally included no fewer than 17 P-40s, Tomahawks and Kittyhawks destroyed.

Born in Friedrichshof, Pomerania, on December 31, 1918, Müncheberg joined the Luftwaffe just shy of his 18th birthday and completed his flight training in late 1937. He received his commission as a leutnant on November 8, 1938 while flying with I./JG 234 at Cologne. Müncheberg was made *gruppe* adjutant with III./JG 26 in September 1939, and he shot down a Blenheim on November 7 for his first victory. Promoted to oberleutnant and serving as *staffelkapitän* of 7./JG 26, Müncheberg fought throughout the Battle of Britain. He had raised his score to 20 victories by September 14, 1940, when he was awarded the *Ritterkreuz* (Knight's Cross).

On February 9, 1941 Müncheberg was ordered to lead his *staffel* to Sicily to bolster the Italian fighter forces that were struggling to gain air superiority over the RAF on Malta. The 14 Bf 109Es of 7. *Staffel*, each adorned with a red heart on its nose, soon swept aside Malta's defending Hurricanes prior to being called away in April to support the invasion of the Balkans. Returning to Maltese skies at month-end, on May 1 Müncheberg claimed three Hurricanes over the embattled island to raise his tally to 41. Later that same month he moved his *staffel* to Greece. The next stop for 7. *Staffel* was Ain el Gazala, Libya, where the unit operated closely with I./JG 27. Müncheberg's score stood at 48 by the time he was ordered to bring 7. *Staffel* back to northern France and rejoin JG 26.

In ten months on the Channel coast, Müncheberg boosted his score to 83 victories while serving as *gruppenkommandeur* of II./JG 26. He finally left the "Schlageter" *Geschwader* on July 21, 1942 for a tour of the Eastern Front in preparation for another promotion, this time to *kommodore* of a *geschwader*. Müncheberg initially served as temporary *kommodore* of JG 51 while Karl-Gottfried Nordmann recovered from a fractured skull, and whilst with the unit he managed to shoot down 33 Russian aircraft to push his score past the 100 mark.

"Jochen" Müncheberg assumed command of JG 77 on October 1, 1942, and promptly relocated his new unit from southern Russia to North Africa. Promoted to major in December, he continued to score steadily while JG 77 took part in the long retreat through Libya and Tunisia. On March 23, 1943, with his score now at 135 victories, Müncheberg engaged a formation of Spitfires from the 52nd FG over Tunisia. Moments after downing one of his opponents, the German ace collided with the fighter flown by Capt Theodore Sweetland, and both pilots crashed to their deaths. In Müncheberg's honor, JG 77 adopted a red heart as its unit badge.

then dive out of the sun on the Allied formations. After a hit-and-run attack, the Luftwaffe pilots would use their superior speed to zoom back up above the enemy for another run.

The P-40, on the other hand, could turn tighter and had superior armament. The best option for Warhawk pilots when confronting the Bf 109 was to try to meet the diving enemy head-on and then lure him into a turning fight. This tactic was so prevalent that one pilot with a sardonic wit in the 64th FS/57th FG christened his P-40 *Messerschmitt Bait*.

German experience in Spain also informed their development of the four-aircraft *Schwarm* as the basic battle formation for fighter-versus-fighter combat. The *Schwarm* consisted of two *Rotten* or loose pairs arrayed roughly line abreast. Within the *Rotte*, the leader was responsible for attacking the enemy and making the kills, while his wingman's duty was to protect the leader's tail. When the Allies later adopted this formation, they named it the "Finger Four" because the aircraft were spread like the fingernails of a person's right hand when viewed from above.

The RAF developed various other formations for use when its Hurricanes and Kittyhawks were operating as fighter-bombers in North Africa, including the "Box Four" for dive-bombing, and American Warhawk squadrons duly followed suit. Fighter-bomber versions of the Bf 109 (called *Jagdbombers* or *Jabos*) also flew in the Mediterranean, but they were displaced by Fw 190 *Jabos* toward the end of the North African campaign.

Largely developed by high-scoring ace Werner Mölders as a result of air combat in Spain, the principal Jagdwaffe fighting formation during World War II was based on the loose *Schwarm* of two *Rotte* of two aircraft. The leader of each pair was covered by his wingman, and the fighters flew far enough apart to allow each pilot to fly in formation with the minimum of effort while concentrating on the sky around them. The *Rotte* supported each other in a similar fashion. Typically, each *Staffel* flew with *Schwarme* in loose line abreast, covering up to a mile of sky.

P-40Fs of the 66th FS/57th FG await take-off orders at Ben Gardane or Soltane, Tunisia, in March 1943.

COMBAT

As the Allied pincers squeezed on Tunisia from the west and south during the spring of 1943, the two remaining *jagdgeschwader* – now equipped with Bf 109Gs – fought doggedly over a steadily shrinking patch of sky. By April, JG 53 *kommodore* Oberst Günther von Maltzahn had begun pulling his units back to the relative safety of Sicily, rather than risk having them trapped in Africa when the inevitable collapse finally happened. JG 77, under the command of Major Johannes Steinhoff, stayed to the bitter end before slipping away to Sicily in the final days prior to Generaloberst Hans-Jürgen von Arnim surrendering all remaining Axis forces to the Allies on May 7.

Having escaped capture, Steinhoff convinced the Luftwaffe to allow his exhausted JG 77 to refit and relax in Italy for several weeks prior to taking up permanent station on Sicily. Although the *jagdgeschwader* had survived with their aircraft and pilots intact, both units had lost vital groundcrews and equipment in the surrender – losses that would prove very difficult for the Luftwaffe to make good at this stage in the war.

Steinhoff recalled his unit's withdrawal from Tunisia in his classic book *The Straits of Messina*:

It had been more like a hasty retreat than a move. The Messerschmitts landed at Trapani on May 8 – they were riddled with bullets and had not been serviced for days. Inside the fuselage of each aircraft knelt a mechanic, a position he had reached with some difficulty by squeezing through the wireless hatch. Without a parachute and with no hope of escaping from his prison in an emergency, he was at the mercy of his fate and his pilot's skill.

The remnants of the group had taken off in dramatic circumstances. The air above Cape Bon – the final bridgehead – was controlled by Allied fighters. We had spent the night beside a small meadow, then, in the short North African spring, an uninterrupted sea of flowers. Our aircraft were able to depart only during intervals when the Spitfires and Kittyhawks were relieving each other. Once airborne, we sought to escape by flying at treetop level. There were dogfights and losses, and columns of smoke from shot-down aircraft marked our course.

USAAF P-40 and Spitfire pilots claimed 11 Bf 109s and one Fi 156 shot down on May 8, and these proved to be their last aerial claims of the North African campaign.

JG 53's *Geschwaderstab* and II. *Gruppe* set up shop at Comiso, with I. *Gruppe* at Catania and III. *Gruppe* at Sciacca, on the southwest coast. Steinhoff placed the *Geschwaderstab* and II. *Gruppe* of JG 77 at the western end of Sicily at Trapani, while I. *Gruppe* went to Sciacca. Three under-strength *Regia Aeronautica* units equipped with Bf 109Gs (3° *Gruppo* C.T., 23° *Gruppo* C.T. and 150° *Gruppo* C.T.) were also based on Sicily, but their operations were not coordinated with those of their Luftwaffe compatriots.

Facing them was an awesome array of Allied fighters and bombers. In addition to five groups of USAAF P-40s and a large wing of RAF Kittyhawks, the fighter force included American and Commonwealth Spitfire squadrons, long-range USAAF P-38 Lightnings and even P-39 Airacobras. However, as Steinhoff makes clear in his book, the primary responsibility of Luftwaffe fighter pilots was to attack and destroy Allied bombers, which included B-17 and B-24 "heavies" and A-20, B-25 and B-26 twin-engined "mediums". Night operations by British bombers would go largely unchallenged.

The stage was now set for the pivotal air battles of the summer, which would shatter the Luftwaffe's fighter force in the Mediterranean and take the *Regia Aeronautica* completely out of the war.

Months before they had wrested North Africa from Axis hands, Allied leaders had begun planning the invasion of Italy. Their first stop on the route through the tragically misnamed "soft underbelly" of Europe would be Sicily, but before that they needed to neutralize the Italian-held island of Pantelleria. Located halfway between the tip of Cape Bon and the coast of Sicily, Pantelleria was a 42-square-mile rock that bristled with observation posts and aerials for direction-finding radios, not to mention heavy fortifications and a large airfield with underground hangars carved into a rock cliff.

The invasion of Sicily, codenamed Operation *Husky*, would be seriously imperiled as long as Pantelleria remained in enemy hands.

Expecting a nasty fight to take Pantelleria, the Allies decided to lay on a heavy aerial campaign against the island to soften it up prior to the sending troops ashore. For these operations, Warhawk units were combined under the command of the Northwest African Air Forces (NAAF), along with medium bomber squadrons of both air forces. The NAAF assault on Pantelleria opened on May 18, 1943, and averaged more than 100 sorties a day through to the

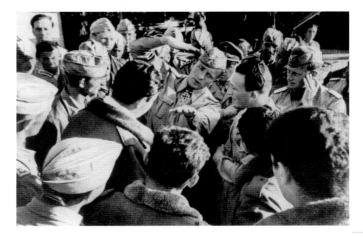

Oberst Günther von Maltzahn, *Kommodore* of JG 53, uses his hands to recount a recent combat to a group of his pilots. It was von Maltzahn's wise decision to begin pulling his unit out of Tunisia in April 1943 before it became trapped there by the Axis surrender.

A Bf 109G-6/trop from II./JG 53, complete with dust filter on the supercharger intake and sun umbrella clamped behind the windscreen, is serviced and refueled between missions on Sicily in the summer of 1943.

end of the month, with little or no aerial opposition from Italian fighter units on the island or the German Bf 109 *gruppen* on Sicily.

When the NAAF stepped up the intensity of its attacks on June 6, 1943, the Luftwaffe finally responded. On an afternoon dive-bombing mission that day, 23 P-40s of the 325th FG were jumped by an equal number of Bf 109s, and six Warhawk pilots were credited with confirmed victories without suffering any losses. One of the victorious pilots, Capt Joe Bloomer of the 318th FS, described the encounter as "duck soup". Pilots of the 57th and 79th FGs submitted claims for two victories each on June 7, and the 33rd FG got into the act two days later when 1Lt Kenneth B. Scidmore of the 60th FS damaged a Bf 109.

The Pantelleria campaign reached its peak on June 10, when NAAF fighters claimed 34 enemy aeroplanes destroyed, three probables and eight damaged. Nearly half of the day's total fell to the 79th FG's 87th FS in a single mission early that afternoon. Arriving off the northeast corner of the island, the 16 Warhawks were flying at 5,000ft when mission leader Lt Col Charles E. Grogan saw a large transport aircraft marked with red crosses flying low over the water, surrounded by ten Bf 109 escorts. It was one of the rare opportunities when P-40s in the MTO were presented with a height advantage over

The 325th FG, at Mateur, Tunisia, was still in the process of marking the tails of its P-40s with a distinctive checker pattern when it began a series of missions against Sardinia during the summer of 1943. Flg Off Bill Slattery of the 318th FS scored three confirmed victories in his P-40F "White 55" *Sweet Laurie* during this period.

Bf 109s, and Grogan made the most of it. Leading his flight downward in a diving attack, Grogan quickly sent a Bf 109 crashing into the water, and each member of his flight – Lts Asa Adair, Kensley Miller and Morris Watkins – followed suit with kills of their own.

Capt Frank M. Huff then spotted a second red cross-marked transport aircraft with a fighter escort and led his flight down in a similar attack. He and Lt Leo Berinati each picked off a Bf 109 close to the water. Capt Lee V. Gossick's flight descended with Huff's and had even more success, Gossick destroying one Messerschmitt and damaging another, while his wingman, Lt Wyman D. Anderson, shot down a pair of C.202s.

Lt Paul McArthur's top cover had also engaged the enemy by this point, with 2Lt John Kirsch diving from 5,000ft to knock down a Bf 109 while McArthur destroyed his second C.202 of the day and two Bf 109s, and also damaged a third "Gustav". That brought the victory tally for the mission to 15 destroyed.

The fight had taken a toll on McArthur's P-40F, however, and his engine began to smoke either from over-exertion by the pilot or a hit from an enemy fighter. McArthur

Allied air power enjoyed vast numerical superiority throughout the softening up and invasion of Sicily in the summer of 1943. P-40s ringed Sicily from their bases in Tunisia and on the islands of Pantelleria and Malta. Tunisia-based P-40s also clashed repeatedly with Bf 109s over Sardinia during this pivotal period.

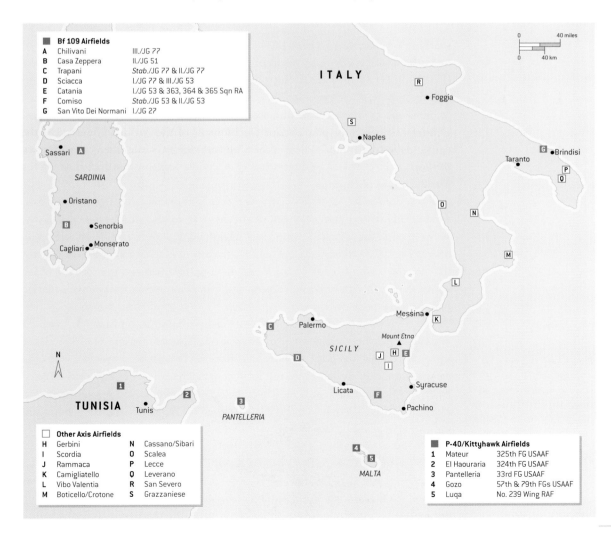

Bf 109 Airfields		
A	Chilivani	III./JG 77
B	Casa Zeppera	II./JG 51
C	Trapani	Stab./JG 77 & II./JG 77
D	Sciacca	I./JG 77 & III./JG 53
E	Catania	I./JG 53 & 363, 364 & 365 Sqn RA
F	Comiso	Stab./JG 53 & II./JG 53
G	San Vito Dei Normani	I./JG 27

ITALY

Other Axis Airfields			
H	Gerbini	N	Cassano/Sibari
I	Scordia	O	Scalea
J	Rammaca	P	Lecce
K	Camigliatello	Q	Leverano
L	Vibo Valentia	R	San Severo
M	Boticello/Crotone	S	Grazzaniese

P-40/Kittyhawk Airfields		
1	Mateur	325th FG USAAF
2	El Haouraria	324th FG USAAF
3	Pantelleria	33rd FG USAAF
4	Gozo	57th & 79th FGs USAAF
5	Luqa	No. 239 Wing RAF

bailed out into the sea 30 miles off the coast of Tunisia and climbed into his half-inflated dinghy while several Warhawks circled overhead to help direct an air-sea rescue aeroplane to him. A soggy McArthur returned to his unit two days later.

II./JG 53, flying from Sicily, also had a productive day on June 10, claiming 15 Allied aircraft destroyed. Among the claims were two P-40s credited to 5. *Staffel* and two Kittyhawks for 8. *Staffel*, one of which was claimed by Oberleutnant Franz Scheiss for his 53rd victory. These four kills all happened at about 1545 hrs, making it likely that they were the result of combat with the 79th FG's 87th FS. In addition, Hauptmann Werner Schroer of *Stab* II./JG 27 claimed two P-40s destroyed that morning for his 78th and 79th victories. The Axis troops on Pantelleria surrendered to the Allies the following day.

ACTION OVER SARDINIA

On June 1 Major Kurt Ubben's III./JG 77 arrived at Chilivani, on the Italian island of Sardinia (some 120 miles north of Tunisia), to bolster its air defenses. Another Bf 109 unit, II./JG 51, was already on the island at Casa Zeppera under Major Karl Rammelt, along with several Italian units equipped with Macchi fighters.

While most of the Allies' attention was focused on Pantelleria following the victory in Africa, other targets beckoned as well. For the 325th FG, which in June had begun painting the tail surfaces of its P-40s with distinctive black and yellow checkers, the summer of 1943 would be dominated by a series of missions northward across the Mediterranean to Sardinia.

It was during the 325th FG's campaign over Sardinia that the "Checkertail Clan" would establish a reputation for prowess in air-to-air combat that survives to this day. Between mid May and late September, Warhawk pilots of the 325th FG racked up no fewer than 102 victories in 37 missions for the loss of just 16 aircraft. In the process, the four pilots who would become aces flying the P-40 with the group in the MTO scored their fifth victories over Sardinia, and several future aces opened their scoring tallies during these sorties too.

The 325th FG flew its first mission to Cagliari, Sardinia, on May 13, 1943, 34 Warhawks escorting bombers northward from the Tunisian coast across 100 miles of sea to the target and back without interference. From this uneventful start, the campaign quickly escalated into full fury six days later when 32 Warhawks escorted B-26s to Decimomannu airfield, where the bombers were to attack a supply depot. Eleven aggressive Bf 109s from II./JG 51 jumped the fighter escorts from above, and soon a big dogfight was underway.

Two future aces of the 325th FG scored their first successes during this engagement, which saw the group claim five victories in total. Maj Robert Baseler of group headquarters and 1Lt Herschel H. "Herky" Green of the 317th FS, who was on his first combat mission, got one apiece. Green only recalled firing a long burst at some passing Bf 109s early on in the fight before two Luftwaffe pilots singled him out.

Flying his P-40 like a combat veteran, rather than the rookie that he was, Green knew his Warhawk could not climb above the Bf 109s or run away from them in level flight. His only choice was to turn into their attacks, and turn he did.

Soon, the Luftwaffe pilots began coordinating their attacks so that if Green turned into one of them, the other would be on his tail. The P-40 took numerous hits, including one 20mm blast in the fuselage that knocked out Green's radio and thudded against the armor plate behind his seat. With his panic rising, Green flipped the Warhawk into an over-the-top snap roll. The fighter stalled, then fell into a power-on spin. It was still spinning when Green reached a layer of clouds and then recovered. Shaken, but unhurt, he nursed the Warhawk back across the sea to his base in Tunisia. Green's fighter was deemed fit only for scrapping. On a more positive note, he learned that his squadron commander, Capt Bill Reed, had seen a Bf 109 go down after Green had fired at it. This was the first of 18 victories that Green would score while flying P-40s, P-47s and P-51s with the 325th FG. He finished the war as the second-highest scoring USAAF ace in the MTO.

The pilots of II./JG 51 claimed no P-40s destroyed on May 19, but that changed the next day. Not satisfied with the results of the bombing from 24 hours earlier, the NAAF ordered a similar mission to Decimomannu on the 20th. This attack proved to be far more successful, and the 325th FG claimed six defending fighters shot down over the target. One of them fell to 1Lt Frank J. "Spot" Collins, this victory being the second of five kills he would score in Warhawks. Then, while returning from the mission, a flight of P-40s led by the group commander, Lt Col Gordon H. Austin, spotted seven Me 323 Gigante transports flying at low altitude and despatched all of the six-engined machines into the sea. Amongst the successes claimed by German fighter pilots on this day was a solitary P-40 for Oberleutnant Horst Walther of *Stab* II./JG 51. His victim was almost certainly Lt Thomas B. Johnson, who ditched his damaged Warhawk in the sea near Toro Island while on the way home.

Now the 325th FG was on a roll, and in six more missions to Sardinia through to the end of June its pilots scored 23 victories. The group spent the first three weeks of July concentrating on supporting the Sicilian invasion. Meanwhile, II./JG 51 scored 17 victories, including seven P-40s, during the same period and two more in early July before being withdrawn to Germany. The *gruppe's* P-40 victories correspond very closely to 325th FG losses during June.

On July 20 the "Checkertails" went back to Sardinia and came home to toast their first ace. Capt Ralph G. "Zack" Taylor shot down two Bf 109s and a C.202 to bring his score to six confirmed – a total that would not be topped until after the group had re-equipped with P-47s in late 1943. III./JG 77, now providing air defense over the island, made no victory claims. This was primarily because the *gruppe* was

II./JG *77*'s Trapani airfield is pounded by Allied bombs in June 1943. The unit was forced to disperse its individual *Staffeln* to smaller landing strips in the surrounding countryside following these attacks on its Sicilian base.

Although one of the signature features of the Warhawk was its ring-and-bead gunsight atop its cowling, the primary sight in the P-40F/L was the USAAF's N-3A reflector gunsight, manufactured by Service Tool Engineering of Dayton, Ohio. The N-3A, like reflector sights used by other combatant air forces during World War II, was essentially a refined ring-and-bead, with the image of the ring-and-bead projected by a light onto a special glass in front of the pilot's eyes so that they were only visible when the pilot was looking directly down the longitudinal axis of his aircraft.

The most important improvement over the ring-and-bead sight was that the reflector's image was focused at infinity, which meant that the pilot did not face the impossible task of trying to focus his sight on two different distances — the sight and the target — at the same time.

The brightness of the image could be adjusted to suit the light conditions. The graticule could also be adjusted to the wingspan of the target aircraft, so when its wings filled the circle the pilot knew he was in range. The graticule was of some help to the pilot in calculating deflection while firing at a target turning away from him, but it was basically no more helpful than a ring-and-bead sight in this regard.

The Warhawk's ring-and-bead sight was included merely as a manual backup in case the reflector sight failed.

now having to field more and more inexperienced fighter pilots as a result of ever mounting losses. Major Johannes Steinhoff, *kommodore* of JG 77, recalled:

> It was no longer possible to introduce the newcomers to the enemy by degrees, for the Spitfires, Warhawks and Lightnings were almost constantly over our airfields. Nor were we able to initiate them into the methods of attacking Fortresses because the closeness of our formation demanded both skill and experience, neither of which they possessed.

More big days followed over Sardinia. Maj Bob Baseler got two of the 325th FG's 17 victories on July 22, and four days later he got one more to bring his total to five,

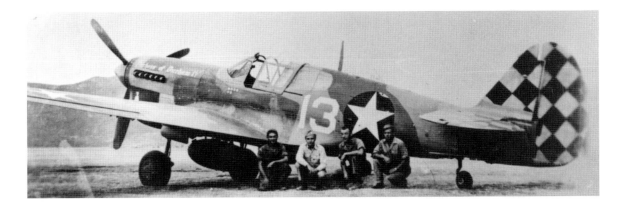

thus making him the second "Checkertail" ace. The 319th FS suffered a sad loss on July 28 when its CO, Capt Everett B. Howe, was shot down by flak. III./JG 77 was able to claim just five victories over Sardinia to this point, none of them P-40s.

The mission on July 30 provided the "Checkertails" with their biggest day of the campaign. It came on a routine sweep over southern Sardinia by 32 P-40s of the 317th and 319th FSs. They were jumped first by 25–30 Bf 109s, and then a second force of "Gustavs" and C.202s piled in. In the ensuing dogfight, the Americans claimed 21 victories for the loss of just one P-40. In the post-mission reports the Warhawk pilots noted that the enemy fighters tried to turn with them, rather than using the normal dive-and-zoom tactics, which may account for the unusually high number of claims. III./JG 77's records show only five losses for the day, but on the other hand its pilots claimed six victories although only one P-40 went down. As might be expected in a widespread engagement involving literally dozens of twisting and turning aircraft, overclaiming of victories seems to have taken place on both sides.

Be that as it may, the 325th FG was awarded a Distinguished Unit Citation for the mission, and it also added another name to its list of aces that day. 1Lt Walter B. "Bud" Walker of the 317th was credited with a triple haul, bringing his total to five. 318th FS pilot Capt John C. A. Watkins wrote the following account of Walker's engagement shortly after the mission:

> "Bud" Walker, a blue squadron flight leader, found himself unaccountably alone, with three Messerschmitts taking turns making passes at him. As one of the little black fighters came down, "Bud" managed to get on his tail, fired long bursts into him and sent him crashing in flames. A second burst into flames in the air and smashed into the olive trees on the valley floor.
>
> Finally, "Bud" found himself only a few feet off the ground, almost scraping his paint off in the olive trees, with only one gun still in action and the third Jerry hanging on his tail and firing round after round of 20mm cannon shells into him. In desperation "Bud" put both hands on the control stick and hauled savagely back into an eye-popping, tight "P-40 turn". The German hauled back, too, trying to turn inside him and finish him off. He never had a chance – his faster and less maneuverable fighter snap rolled into the ground and burned.

Ace Capt Ralph G. "Zack" Taylor claimed five of his six victories in this P-40L-1 (42-10436), which was nicknamed *Duchess of Durham IV/My Gal Sal*. Taylor, kneeling second from left, was credited with destroying four Bf 109s and two C.202s. His final three successes came on July 20, 1943 north of Monserrato airfield, on the island of Sardinia.

"Bud" was officially credited with three kills, the last without firing a shot. He came home with great gaping holes in the fuselage of his ship, torn by bursting shells. His legs were scratched and powder-burned from the heavy machine gun bullets which had riddled the cockpit.

Six III./JG 77 pilots each claimed one P-40 destroyed, namely Oberleutnant Erhart Niese of 7 *Staffel* (his 15th victory), Feldwebel Hans-Werner Renzow of 8 *Staffel* and Oberleutnant Wolfgang Ernst (his 25th victory), Leutnant Gerhard Bertram, Unteroffiziere Walther Barten and Jürgen Baesler, all of 9 *Staffel*.

The 325th FG's final aerial victories over Sardinia – and, in fact, its final aerial claims in P-40s – came on August 28 during a dive-bombing mission against a factory at Fluminimaggiore. As was so often the case, the Warhawk pilots were jumped from above and behind, but were able to turn the tables on their attackers. Jettisoning their bombs and turning into the attack, the top-cover P-40s claimed seven destroyed, with just two of their own damaged. Capt Frank J. "Spot" Collins was credited with one Bf 109 destroyed, bringing his total to five and making him the last P-40 ace of the 325th FG. Oberleutnante Niese and Ernst and Feldwebel Schmitz claimed Warhawks destroyed for III./JG 77.

The "Checkertails" flew six more missions to Sardinia, capping off the campaign with an uneventful sweep over the island on September 14. A week later Axis forces on Sardinia surrendered, and two days after that the 325th FG stood down to begin its transition to the massive Republic P-47 Thunderbolt. Its Warhawks were spread among the four remaining P-40 groups in the MTO, their black-and-yellow checkered tails painted out with a drab coat of camouflage.

Capt Watkins summed up the 325th's campaign over Sardinia as follows:

Veteran fighter pilot Major Johannes "Macki" Steinhoff saw combat throughout the war, completing 939 missions and being credited with 176 victories. Given command of JG 77 in March 1943, he led the unit in North Africa and then through the maelstrom of air combat over Sicily and Italy. Having claimed four Soviet P-40s destroyed in 1942 whilst leading II./JG 52 on the Eastern Front, Steinhoff became a Curtiss fighter ace when he downed a USAAF Warhawk on July 8, 1943.

Capt Walter "Bud" Walker of the 317th FS/325th FG (center), seen here with his groundcrew and his P-40F "White 25", was one of several 325th FG pilots who reached ace status during the Sardinia missions, scoring his fifth victory on July 30, 1943.

Ours was strictly a gentleman's war. We set our own time and place to fight. We ranged up and down the island, staging dogfights in the best Hollywood style when we – by dropping fragmentation bombs on their aerodromes – made their fighters mad enough to come up and fight us. We dive-bombed power stations, bridges and factories, strafed air raid warning stations along the coast and attacked enemy ships whenever one of them attempted a rare dash down the coast in daylight.

OPERATION *HUSKY*

While the aerial campaigns against Pantelleria and Sardinia were spectacular and successful, the Allies' invasion of Sicily was the high point of the war in the MTO during the summer of 1943. The NAAF threw its full force into the process of softening up Sicily, starting as soon as Pantelleria fell. Massive formations of medium and heavy bombers, covered by swarms of fighters, ranged over Sicily from late June, attacking airfields, lines of transportation and communications, supply depots and anything else they could find of military value. Axis fighter units on the island responded as best they could, but they were greatly outnumbered and doomed to failure.

Hoping to delay the invasion, General Adolf Galland – sent to Sicily to organize the fighter defenses – planned a mass assault by Bf 109s against the Allied bombers now attacking the island on a daily basis. The mission took place on June 25, but it proved to be an abject failure as the Bf 109s got caught between a high-altitude B-17 strike and a low-level raid by B-26s. Major Johannes Steinhoff brought down a single B-17 for the only claim of the day.

On learning the news, an enraged Reichsmarschall Hermann Göring, commander-in-chief of the Luftwaffe, sent a telex threatening to court martial a pilot from each of the *jagdgruppen* involved in the mission for cowardice. Now, in addition to being outnumbered and fatigued, the Bf 109 pilots on Sicily were demoralized as well. The fact that Göring's threat was never carried out did nothing to improve the situation.

Of the NAAF P-40 units involved in the pre-invasion missions over Sicily, the 324th FG, operating as an independent unit for the first time and with the all-black 99th FS attached, saw the most action. The group's three squadrons – the 314th, 315th and 316th FSs – reunited on June 18 at El Houaria, on Cape Bon. After a week of flying defensive patrols over Pantelleria, the group was ordered out on a fighter sweep over southern Sicily on July 1. For two weeks after that, such missions became a daily chore for the 324th FG pilots. One such individual was 1Lt Sidney W. Brewer of the 315th FS, who recounted his experience in a privately published memoir:

The pre-invasion sorties we flew over Sicily were undoubtedly the most dangerous of all my combat flying. Each mission involved a long 150-mile overwater flight, which gave the Germans plenty of time to prepare a proper reception for us, and they did. We flew

OVERLEAF
Tasked with holding the Luftwaffe on Sardinia at bay during the Sicily invasion, the 325th FG sent 32 Warhawks on a sweep of the island on July 30, 1943. Bf 109Gs from 7. and 9./JG 77 were scrambled from their base at Chilivani and bounced the 317th FS over Oristano. A large swirling dogfight erupted, and Italian C.202s and C.205s of 51° *Stormo* joined in as the battle moved southward down the center of the island. One of the P-40 pilots, Lt Walter "Bud" Walker, "Blue" Flight leader, found himself alone with three Bf 109s that took it in turns to make firing passes at him. Despite being outnumbered, Walker managed to get onto the tail of one of the "Gustavs" and fire a long burst into it, sending the fighter down in flames. He then targeted a second machine, which crashed into olive trees on the valley floor. Finally, at extreme low altitude, and with just one gun continuing to fire, Walker was set upon by the third Bf 109, which pumped several cannon shells into the fuselage of his P-40. In desperation, Walker yanked his Warhawk into a maximum rate turn. The Bf 109 pilot tried to follow but his fighter snap-rolled and crashed. Walker had scored his third kill of the day without firing a shot. In all, the P-40 pilots claimed to have destroyed 21 enemy aircraft, with four probables. One P-40 was shot down. In reality, III./JG 77 had lost five Bf 109s that day, while claiming five Warhawks destroyed in return. Whatever the case, the 325th FG was awarded a Distinguished Unit Citation for the mission.

Capt John C. A. Watkins of the 325th FG HQ poses with his crew chief, Sgt Misenheimer, and their P-40L-5 42-10866 "White 59" *BIG HELEN III* in September 1943. Watkins, who wrote a number of detailed stories on the exploits of his group, was credited with gaining permission for the 325th FG to apply the checkerboard marking to the tails of its aircraft.

72-ship formations, and we had some success, but they too had success. By and large, we suffered more losses than they did.

Frequently, 100+ German fighters would intercept us, and grand air battles were almost a daily event. We soon wore them down, however, and their attacks on us were less and less effective in ever decreasing numbers. By July 10, when our ground forces landed in Sicily, we had obtained complete mastery of the air. The period July 1 until July 16 proved to be the most crucial of all my experiences to that time. I flew 12 missions to Sicily, many involving night take-offs so as to be there at first light. Our losses were heavy. For example, on July 8 we lost ten pilots and as many aeroplanes, including *Brittle II*, which was my machine. She went into the ocean after one of our guys bailed out of her. Later that day I got a new aeroplane, and it was destroyed when I had to belly in upon returning from a mission. It was a hard two weeks, and we were all tired and combat-weary by the end of it.

The 324th FG had a tough time over Sicily, losing nine pilots in two weeks, including the 316th FS CO, Maj Bob Dempsey. But the group also inflicted its share of damage on the Axis defenders, destroying 21 enemy fighters between July 2 and 10. Several of the group's pilots, including Capt Bruce Hunt and 1Lt Andrew D'Antoni of the 314th FS and 1Lt Charles Harrington of the 316th FS, were awarded Distinguished Flying Crosses for individual acts of bravery during the period. In addition, the pilot who would become the 324th FG's last ace, 1Lt James E. "Murph" Fenex, was leading a flight of 316th FS when he scored his first two kills on July 9.

Bf 109G pilots of II./JG 77 claimed six P-40s and/or Kittyhawks destroyed on this date, with two being credited to Hauptmann Siegfried Freytag for his 97th and 98th victories. Four more Kittyhawks were claimed by JG 53, including one by Oberfeldwebel Herbert Rollwage of 5. *Staffel* for his 45th victory.

On July 10, the Warhawk pilots at El Houaria were awakened long before daylight to prepare for the mission they had been anticipating for two weeks. P-40s were ordered off at 0425 hrs to provide cover for the Allied landings on Sicily – the big show was on, and the 324th FG would be in the thick of it. The group flew a series of escort missions for C-47 transports en route to Sicily through to the end of July, and then it returned to Causeway LG, Tunisia, where it would remain inactive until October.

Bf 109 pilots were busy on the opening day of the invasion as well, II./JG 77 claiming five Kittyhawks in two combats and Leutnant Karl Paashus of 5./JG 53 adding a P-40 at 1035 hrs for his sixth victory of the war. But these successes failed to satisfy a by-now thoroughly rattled Reichsmarschall Hermann Göring, who fired off another telex on the evening of July 11:

This replacement Bf 109G-6 on Sicily still bears the factory-applied identification letters under its wing, although it has also been marked with the red-heart badge of JG 77. "Macki" Steinhoff's unit did its best to defend Sicily from Allied air attacks, but was forced to withdraw to Italy on July 13, 1943.

Together with the fighter pilots in France, Norway and Russia, I look with scorn upon the pilots in the south. I want to see an immediate improvement, and expect all pilots to display more fighting spirit. Should this improvement not be forthcoming, all pilots

Crew chief Sgt Edward Champion runs up the engine of well-worn P-40F-15 "Y76" (41-19736), the regular mount of Lt "Bucky" Buchanan of the 316th FS/ 324th FG in the summer of 1943. The group flew numerous missions during the softening up of Sicily in preparation for the July 10, 1943 invasion.

A vine-leaf garlanded Oberfeldwebel Herbert Rollwage of 5./JG 53 clutches a cactus plant in a bomb tail "vase" after returning to Comiso on August 8, 1942 upon the completion of his 300th mission. By war's end he had increased that number to 664 missions, and claimed as many as 85 victories. Rollwage's sole P-40 success came on July 9, 1943 during the doomed defense of Sicily.

— from *kommodores* downwards — must expect to be reduced to the rank of aircraftsman and sent to serve as infantry on the eastern front.

But to those facing the daily reality of overwhelming enemy superiority in the air, and constant bombardment on the ground, the Reichsmarschall's empty and increasingly irrational threats now counted for little. For by this time II./JG 53 was already preparing to evacuate its damaged but still airworthy "Gustavs" across the Straits of Messina to mainland Italy, where they were to be hurriedly replaced by a new complement of Bf 109G-6s.

This Bf 109G-6/trop was found by the 65th FS/57th FG when the unit arrived at its first airfield in Sicily. One of dozens of abandoned Axis fighters left on the island, the "Gustav" was quickly repaired, repainted and flown by several pilots, including Capt Jim Hadnot.

The 33rd FG moved its P-40s to Pantelleria after the Italians surrendered the island on June 11, 1943. The rocky hillside in the foreground shelters a fortified aircraft hangar that the Americans put to good use keeping their fighters maintained during the ensuing aerial assault on Sicily.

While the 324th FG was flying its missions from Cape Bon to Sicily, the 33rd FG was performing similar duties from its newly captured base on Pantelleria. The 57th and 79th FGs were not employed until after the July 10 landings. Once the Allied ground forces began to advance on Sicily, the Luftwaffe fighter units were forced to withdraw to landing grounds in Italy. The rest of the campaign was primarily fighter-bomber work, although two more P-40 pilots reached ace status during this period – Maj John Bradley, CO of the 58th FS/33rd FG, and 1Lt Paul G. McArthur of the 87th FS/79th FG, his group's only ace of the war.

The NAAF had already begun its softening-up air campaign against mainland Italy when the remaining Axis forces on Sicily surrendered on August 17, 1943. By this time, three P-40 groups – the 33rd, 57th and 79th FGs – were operating from Sicilian airfields, while the 324th FG remained inactive in Tunisia and the 325th FG completed its campaign against Sardinia, prior to giving up its Warhawks. Meanwhile, the Ninth Air Force departed for England to become the tactical air component of the cross-channel invasion force, and its three P-40 groups shifted to command of the Twelfth Air Force.

The British Eighth Army's XIII Corps crossed the Straits of Messina on September 3, 1943 to make an amphibious landing at Calabria, on the toe of Italy. The main Allied landings took place six days later at Salerno and Taranto, thus opening a new phase in the war.

P-40s and Bf 109s would continue to have occasional encounters in the MTO for the next nine months as the Warhawk was gradually phased out and the Luftwaffe slowly withdrew its fighter units from Italy one by one. These combats would never again reach the level of intensity that the opposing pilots experienced during the summer of 1943, however.

STATISTICS AND ANALYSIS

A statistical analysis comparing the relative success or failure of the P-40F/L versus the Bf 109F/G in the MTO is all but impossible. Both types contributed significantly to their national war efforts, but in different ways. The key point to remember is that the P-40 flew primarily in a fighter-bomber role, while most Bf 109s were employed as pure aerial interceptors and fought against multiple Allied fighter types, not just Warhawks.

There is no disputing that the Bf 109 enjoyed certain performance advantages over the P-40 in aerial combat. As long as the Messerschmitt pilot was able to stick with the Luftwaffe's tried-and-true tactics of diving from superior height when attacking and then zooming back above the enemy after his firing pass, he had a high likelihood of success. Still, an analysis by the author of victory claims on both sides reveals a slightly different story.

The five USAAF fighter groups that operated the P-40 in the MTO claimed a total of 592 aerial victories with their Warhawks, of which 321 victims were Bf 109s. Conversely, the five Bf 109 *jagdgeschwader* that claimed P-40 victories in the region compiled a grand total of 1,118 Curtiss fighters destroyed! Of these, 486 were shot down before the first USAAF P-40s arrived in the MTO. That lowers the victory ratio of Luftwaffe Bf 109 pilots versus USAAF Warhawk pilots to slightly less than two-to-one. However, the RAF continued flying Kittyhawks after the Americans arrived in-theater, and certainly contributed a substantial number of the 632 P-40 kills registered by the Luftwaffe after mid-August 1942. Considering these numbers, it would be very difficult to argue that the fighter pilots of one side or the other were superior, although the high scores of various Luftwaffe *experten* might suggest otherwise unless viewed in this context.

American-flown P-40s were just one element of the massive Allied air fleet that battered the Luftwaffe in the Mediterranean during the summer of 1943. Individual achievements by Luftwaffe Bf 109 pilots defending Pantelleria, Sicily and Sardinia were laudable but simply insufficient to hold back the tide of Allied air power. According to author Karl Toll, who writes extensively about the Luftwaffe, the Luftwaffe lost 711 aircraft in the Mediterranean during July 1943 alone. The 246

JG 27 took by far the heaviest toll on P-40s among *jagdgeschwader* in the Mediterranean, its pilots being credited with 676 victories over various versions of the Curtiss fighter. Here, a *schwarm* of 7. *Staffel* "Gustavs" led by 27-victory ace Ltn Josef-Emil Clade (closest to camera) escort a VIP transport over the Aegean Sea in late 1943. Clade claimed four P-40 kills in 1942.

fighters – mostly Bf 109s – among the losses represented fully 13 percent of the Luftwaffe's entire fighter inventory. It was a blow with worldwide implications, for the Luftwaffe never recovered.

ACES' LISTS

The lists below include the names of outstanding P-40 and Bf 109 pilots who flew in the MTO, but they do not present comparable information about the success of the two fighter types in combat against each other due to the variables discussed previously in this chapter. The tallies listed below are based on the victory claims attributed to the pilots at the time this book was written, and are subject to change if further information comes to light.

P-40 ACES WITH Bf 109 VICTORIES IN THE MTO 1942–44				
Name	Unit	Bf 109 Victories	Total P-40 Score	Notes
Maj Levi R. Chase	33rd FG	6	10	+2 kills in P-51
1Lt Robert J. Byrne	57th FG	6	6	
Capt Frank J. Collins	325th FG	5	5	+4 kills in P-47
Capt Lyman Middleditch Jr	57th FG	5	5	First MTO ace
1Lt Robert J. Overcash	57th FG	5	5	
1Lt Walter B. Walker Jr	325th FG	5	5	
Capt Ralph G. Taylor Jr	325th FG	4	7	
Col William W. Momyer	33rd FG	3	8	
Maj John L. Bradley	33rd FG	3	5	
1Lt Paul G. McArthur	79th FG	3	5	
Capt Herschel H. Green	325th FG	3	3	+10 kills in P-47 & 5 in P-51
Capt Roy E. Whittaker	57th FG	2	7	
Capt James E. Fenex Jr	324th FG	2	5	
2Lt George P. Novotny	325th FG	2	3	+5 kills in P-47
Maj Robert L. Baseler	325th FG	1	6	
2Lt MacArthur Powers	324th FG	1	5	+2.25 kills in RAF
Maj Mark E. Hubbard	33rd FG	1	4	+2.5 kills in P-38
2Lt Alfred C. Froning	57th FG	1	3	+2 kills in P-47
2Lt Roy B. Hogg	325th FG	1	2	+2 kills in P-47 & 2 in P-51
Flt Off Cecil O. Dean	325th FG	1	1	+3 kills in P-47 & 2 in P-51
2Lt Richard W. Dunkin	325th FG	1	1	+3 kills in P-47 & 5 in P-51

LEADING Bf 109 ACES WHO SHOT DOWN P-40s IN THE MTO 1941–44 (50+ VICTORIES)

Name	Unit	P-40 Victories	Total Score	Notes
Hptm Hans-Joachim Marseille	JG 27	101	158	KIA 30/9/42
Ltn Werner Schroer	JG 27	40	114	
Hptm Heinz Bär	JG 77	38	220	
Ltn Ernst-Wilhelm Reinert	JG 77	30	174	
Ofw Otto Schulz	JG 27	30	51	KIA 17/6/42
Oblt Gustav Rödel	JG 27	29	98	
Ltn Hans-Arnold Stahlschmidt	JG 27	28	59	KIA 7/9/42
Maj Joachim Müncheberg	JGs 26 & 77	17	135	KIA 23/3/43
Hptm Heinz-Edgar Berres	JG 77	14	52	KIA 24/7/43
Hptm Anton Hackl	JG 77	12	192	
Oblt Fritz Geisshardt	JG 77	8	102	
Oblt Siegfried Freytag	JG 77	8	102	
Hptm Kurt Ubben	JG 77	7	111	
Oblt Emil Omert	JG 77	6	70	
Ofw Herbert Kaiser	JG 77	6	68	
Ltn Fritz Dinger	JG 53	4	67	KIA 23/11/42
Ofw Alexander Preinfalk	JG 77	3	85	
Ltn Wolfgang Tonne	JG 53	2	122	KIA 20/4/43
Oblt Erbo Graf von Kageneck	JG 27	2	67	KIA 23/12/41
Maj Johannes Steinhoff	JG 77	1	176	
Ltn Wilhelm Crinius	JG 53	1	114	PoW 13/1/43
Maj Hartman Grasser	JG 51	1	103	

AFTERMATH

With their personnel exhausted and their supplies of Bf 109Gs drastically depleted, the remains of JGs 53 and 77 pulled out of Sicily on July 13, 1943 – just three days after the Operation *Husky* landings – and set off in unorganized fashion for safe haven in Italy.

Major Johannes Steinhoff recalled the day in his book *The Straits of Messina*. After watching helplessly on the ground as a formation of B-26s made an unsuccessful attack on the airfield at Trapani, the weary *kommodore* of JG 77 considered the evacuation order he had received that morning:

Groundcrews played a vital role on both sides during the air war in the MTO. Here, armorers of the 315th FS/ 324th FG clean the 0.50-in. machine guns of one of the squadron's P-40s on a cold winter's day in December 1943 at Cercola, in Italy.

I wondered what to do next, and I decided there was nothing for me to do but relax in my deck chair under the awning outside the hut and wait until the work of destruction was complete and everything had been burned, blown up or smashed to smithereens. It was absolutely pointless to attempt any further sorties. I would watch them take off one after the other to fly to the mainland and then I would be free, relieved of responsibility – for a few days I'd be out of contact, out of action, out of service and out of the running.

Once again the bombers would lay waste to this already scarred landscape, bringing home to the Sicilians the fact that our last hour had come.

After taking a few days to relax and reorganize, Steinhoff's *Stab.*/JG 77 began operations from Camigliatello, on the extreme "toe" of the Italian "boot" on the Straits of Messina. I./JG 77, commanded by Major Heinz Bär, was just up the coast at Vibo Valentia, and Major Siegfried

Freytag's II. *Gruppe* went to Botricello/Crotone, on the far side of the "toe". III./JG 77, meanwhile, would remain on Sardinia until September 10, then go to Corsica briefly, before transferring to Rumania.

JG 53, with its *kommodore* Oberst Günther von Maltzahn, used Vibo Valentia as its headquarters for several weeks before moving north to Camaldoli, near Naples. Hauptmann Friedrich-Karl Müller moved I./JG 53 from Vibo Valentia to San Severo, on the Foggia plain, on July 16. II. *Gruppe*, under Hauptmann Gerhard Michalski, and III.

Gruppe, under Hauptmann Franz Götz, flew briefly from Lecce, on the "heel" of the "boot", before moving north to the Naples area. Meanwhile, II./JG 27 arrived at Brindisi and flew sorties over Sicily for several weeks before handing over its Bf 109Gs to the remaining *gruppen* and returning to Germany to re-equip.

The British Eighth Army opened the invasion of Italy on September 3, 1943 with landings on the "toe" of the nation's "boot" at Reggio di Calabria. Just five days later the Italian government capitulated, having deposed dictator Benito Mussolini in late July. Now with German forces as their only foe, the Allies staged two more landings, at Taranto and Salerno, on September 9.

The successful Allied landings forced the Luftwaffe fighter units to evacuate yet again. JGs 53 and 77 initially withdrew to airfields near Foggia, and then began a series of moves that would take them steadily northward over the next nine months.

The three P-40 groups on Sicily provided support for the invasion forces by flying patrols and escorting medium bombers attacking German lines of communication. Up to this point, Warhawk pilots had found little air opposition over Italy. Finally, on August 26, a flight of P-40Ls from the 59th FS/33rd FG scored the Warhawk's first victories over the mainland when they claimed three Bf 109s destroyed and two probables near Lamezia. Two pilots from II./JG 53 claimed P-40s shot down, but in fact no Warhawks were lost.

Against a scenic Alpine backdrop in northern Italy, Hauptmann Jürgen Harder, *Gruppenkommandeur* of I./JG 53, checks to see how work is progressing on his Bf 109G-6 "gunboat" (note the port underwing cannon gondola lying on the ground at front right) in the spring of 1944. Harder's I. *Gruppe* left Italy for Rumania on May 1, never to return.

By the spring of 1944, crew chief William Holenchak of the 316th FS/324th FG had proudly painted 110 mission symbols on his P-40F-15 41-19893. Christened *"ANNE"*, the aircraft is seen here loaded with a 500lb bomb on the centerline and three 40lb weapons beneath each wing. The 324th FG was the last USAAF unit to fly the P-40 in the MTO, converting to P-47s in July 1944.

P-40 pilot Lt Dave Giltner of the 315th FS/324th FG straddles a pair of 500lb bombs on an airfield in Italy. Although the P-40 did its share of air-to-air fighting in the MTO, its pilots claiming nearly 600 enemy aircraft shot down, the Warhawk was used primarily as a fighter-bomber.

The next encounter came on invasion day, September 3, when the 57th FG sent 24 Warhawks from the 64th and 65th FSs to escort B-25s attacking enemy positions at Camigliatello. Lt Paul Carll, flying P-40 "38" in the 64th FS "Red" Section, claimed one Bf 109 destroyed.

The Salerno invasion, code-named Operation *Avalanche*, did not go well during the first few days, but by September 13 the ground forces had secured the airfield at Montecorvino and the Warhawks of the 33rd FG moved in immediately. Now the group's P-40 pilots found themselves in the thick of the fighting, with their primary objective being to defend the Salerno beachhead from raiding Luftwaffe fighter-bombers.

The 33rd FG's unofficial history, *Combat Digest*, described this period as follows:

The German Air Force was very much alive again, and usually made three raids per day at breakfast, lunch and dinner, plus the night raids. They would come in from the sea, dive-bomb the shipping and pass over the field on their way home, sometimes firing but in too big of a hurry to do much damage. The group's patrols would jump the Jerries as soon as they came off the bomb run and through the terrific barrage of flak from our ship and shore batteries. After about five days of suffering heavy losses, the Jerry raids slowed down and finally ceased altogether, except for the night raids.

The 33rd FG pilots, highly experienced and spoiling for a good scrap, acquitted themselves well over Salerno. In three days – September 15–17 – they were credited with destroying 14 Bf 109s and Fw 190s for the loss of just a single P-40. These kills were spread among all three squadrons of the group, with the top scorer being 2Lt Morgan S. Tyler of the 59th FS with two victories. Neither JGs 53 nor 77 filed any claims for P-40s destroyed during this period.

The 57th and 79th FGs took up station on the Italian mainland on September 15. Both groups were assigned to support the British invasion force pushing north from

P-47Ds began replacing Warhawks in the Twelfth Air Force from late 1943, with this particular Thunderbolt (which carried the name *Yinn Fiss* on both sides of the forward fuselage) being assigned to Lt Jimmie R. Long Jr of the 65th FS/57th FG.

Taranto, and in short order they found themselves moving to bases on the Foggia Plain that had recently been evacuated by Luftwaffe fighter units. At this point, the Allied advance in southern Italy ground to a halt. Generalfeldmarschall Albert Kesselring, commander of German forces in Italy, used the rugged terrain to his advantage and managed to establish a defensive barrier across the Italian peninsula roughly 80 miles south of Rome. Called the "Gustav Line", it stretched from just north of Naples on the west coast to the Trigno River on the east. P-40 Warhawks would spend the rest of their tenure in the MTO aiding the bloody effort to break through the "Gustav Line".

The remaining P-40 units of the Twelfth Air Force moved to Italy in late October. The 324th FG made its new home at Cercola LG, at the foot of Mt Vesuvius near Naples, and the 99th FS joined the 79th FG at Foggia No 3 LG.

With the stalemate developing on the ground and the Luftwaffe now operating from bases north of Rome, Warhawk squadrons in Italy once again found themselves operating as long-range artillery in the fighter-bomber mode, with little opportunity for aerial combat. The experience of the 314th FS/324th FG was typical. From the date of its first mission out of Cercola (October 20) through to the end of the 1943, the 314th FS flew 64 missions, and on every one of them the Warhawks were loaded with 500lb or 1,000lb bombs. Following the 33rd FG's flurry of air combat over the Salerno beachhead, P-40 pilots in Italy scored only 15 more victories before the end of the year. Now, German flak and the frequently poor Italian winter weather were the pilots' biggest worries.

The American invasion at Anzio on January 22, 1944, designed to break the stalemate on the "Gustav Line", provided one last flurry of aerial combat for P-40 pilots of the Twelfth Air Force. Allied intelligence estimated that the Luftwaffe had about 300 fighters within striking distance of Anzio, which is on the west coast of Italy some 25 miles south of Rome, so plans were made to establish a constant umbrella of fighters over the invasion beach to provide air defense. Spitfires would provide high cover, while P-40s of the 33rd, 79th and 324th FGs would patrol below 12,000ft.

Spitfires duly drove off the opening attack by bomb-carrying Fw 190s at first light on D-Day. Then, at midday, the Warhawks got into the action when 16 P-40Ls of the

An unknown pilot of 8./JG 53 prepares to take off from Villa Orba airfield, in Italy, in well-worn Bf 109G-6 "Black 16" during the battle for the Anzio beachhead in the spring of 1944.

87th FS/79th FG took on a gaggle of Fw 190s and Bf 109s just north of Anzio and knocked down six for the loss of a single Warhawk. II./JG 77 claimed two Spitfires and a B-25 destroyed that day, but no P-40s.

Similar engagements continued for a week, and by the end of January Warhawk pilots of the three groups had claimed 45 victories over Anzio.

By the spring of 1944 time was catching up with the old P-40. The last Merlin-powered Warhawk – P-40L-20 42-11129 – had rolled off the Curtiss assembly line in April 1943, and the USAAF did not consider the Allison-powered P-40N suitable for combat against the Luftwaffe. With production of the big Republic P-47D Thunderbolt, which showed promise as a fighter-bomber, by now in high gear, the fighter was chosen as a successor to the P-40. In mid-December 1943, the 57th and 325th FGs flew their first missions with the Thunderbolt. The 79th FG would follow in March 1944, and with the 33rd FG transferring to China that same month, only the 324th FG (with the 99th FS now attached) would remain as a Warhawk outfit.

Two pilots from JG 53 had the distinction of officially claiming the last victories over P-40s in the Mediterranean. Unteroffizier Günther Landt of 8. *Staffel* claimed a

Having been the first Luftwaffe fighter unit to see action on Sardinia from May 1943, II./JG 51 moved to Sicily the following month. By the time this photograph of 4. *Staffel's* "White 7" (flown by Leutnant Elias Kühlein) was taken some 12 months later, the *gruppe* was flying from Nis, in Yugoslavia.

Bf 109s continued to fly in the three *gruppi* of the Italian ANR after the Luftwaffe pulled its fighters out of Italy in the summer of 1944. Here, an ANR C.205 formates on Bf 109G-6 "White 3" of 4./JG 77 over northern Italy shortly before the latter unit departed for Germany.

P-40 on March 19, 1944 and Unteroffizier Paul Mang of 9. *Staffel* closed out the score with a Kittyhawk shot down on April 7. Mang's claim was the 1,118th for a Tomahawk, Kittyhawk or P-40 in the Mediterranean since mid-1941!

On May 13 P-40s tangled with German fighters for the last time. Lts James Dealy and William King of the 316th FS were involved, and each pilot was credited with shooting down a Bf 109, as was Lt Ken Scheiwe of the 315th FS. Dealy and Lt Arthur Kusch were shot down, however, the former being befriended by partisans who helped him evade capture and return to his squadron. JG 53 claimed two P-47s shot down on this date but no P-40s.

The 324th FG was transferred to the Anzio beachhead on June 6, 1944, and a week later it moved again, this time to an airfield north of Rome. It was from this field, Monalto di Castro, that the group flew its last P-40 missions on July 18, 1944. Immediately thereafter the pilots flew their combat-weary aeroplanes to Naples and traded them for new P-47Ds. The Warhawk's long war in the MTO was over.

JG 53 had left Italy by this time, having pulled out for Germany the previous month. JG 77 continued to fly missions from its base at Villa Franca, in the far north of Italy, for another month, however. Surviving records suggest that the last two Luftwaffe Bf 109 victories in Italy were credited to Leutnant Erich Mühleise of *Stab* II./JG 77 when he claimed a P-51 on July 18 and a B-24 two days later.

This was not the end of combat for the Bf 109 in Italy though. Despite the fact that the country's fascist government had surrendered in September 1943, a new Italian air force with an allegiance to dictator Benito Mussolini was formed a month later after Il Duce's rescue from an Allied prison. Units of the *Aeronautica Nazionale Repubblicana* (ANR) initially flew the Macchi C.205 and Fiat G.55 in defense of the industrial cities in northern Italy. As supplies of these aircraft dwindled, the Luftwaffe began re-equipping the ANR with Bf 109Gs, and by mid-1944 the transition was complete. The Bf 109 pilots of the ANR's three *gruppi* fought until the end of the war in Europe, claiming 226 aerial victories in the face of overwhelming odds.

FURTHER READING

BOOKS

Angelucci, Enzo, *The Rand McNally Encyclopedia of Military Aircraft* (The Military Press, 1983)

Bowman, Martin, *Osprey Duel 11 – P-47 Thunderbolt vs Bf 109G/K, Europe 1943–45* (Osprey Publishing, 2008)

Craig, Harry W. (editor), *The Odyssey of the 324th Fighter Group* (Printel, 1945)

Holmes, Tony, *Osprey Duel 5 – Spitfire vs Bf 109, Battle of Britain* (Osprey Publishing, 2007)

Johnson, Frederick A., *P-40 Warhawk* (MBI Publishing Company, 1998)

Knoke, Heinz, *I Flew for the Führer* (Paperback Library Inc., 1967)

Kupferer, Anthony J., *The Story of the 58th Fighter Group in World War II* (Taylor Publishing Co., 1989)

McDowell, Ernest R., *Checkertails* (Squadron/Signal Publications, 1994)

Molesworth, Carl, *Osprey Aircraft of the Aces 43 – P-40 Warhawk Aces of the MTO* (Osprey Publishing, 2002)

Molesworth, Carl, *Osprey Duel 8 – P-40 Warhawk vs Ki-43 "Oscar", 1944–45* (Osprey Publishing, 2008)

Molesworth, Carl, *Osprey Aviation Elite Units 39 – 57th Fighter Group, "First in the Blue"* (Osprey Publishing, 2011)

Musciano, Walter A., *Messerschmitt Aces* (Arco Publishing Company Inc., 1982)

Olynyk, Frank J., *USAAF (Mediterranean Theater) Credits for the Destruction of Enemy Aircraft* (Frank J. Olynyk, 1987)